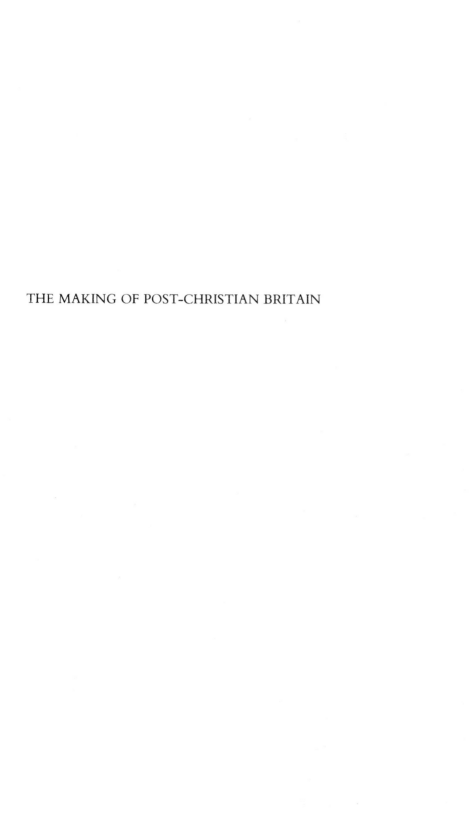

THE MAKING OF POST-CHRISTIAN BRITAIN

# The Making of Post-Christian Britain

A history of the secularization of modern society

*Alan D. Gilbert*

*Longman*
London and New York

**Longman Group Limited** London

*Longman House*
*Burnt Mill, Harlow, Essex, UK*

*Published in the United States of America*
*by Longman Inc., New York*

*First published 1980*

**British Library Cataloguing in Publication Data**

Gilbert, Alan D
   The making of Post-Christian Britain.
   1. Secularism – Great Britain – History
   I. Title
   301.5'8   BL2765.G7   80-40074

   ISBN 0-582-48563-0
   ISBN 0-582-48564-9 Pbk

Set in 10/12 pt V-I-P Bembo
Printed in Great Britain by
Richard Clay (The Chaucer Press) Ltd,
Bungay, Suffolk.

*For Ingrid,*
*Michelle and Fiona*

# Contents

# Preface and acknowledgements

A post-Christian society is not one from which Christianity has departed, but one in which it has become marginal. It is a society where to be irreligious is to be normal, where to think and act in secular terms is to be conventional, where neither status nor respectability depends upon the practice or profession of religious faith. Some members of such a society continue to find Christianity a profound, vital influence in their lives, but in so doing they place themselves outside the mainstream of social life and culture. Like the early Christians in a pre-Christian, classical world, they become a 'peculiar people', anomalous in their primary beliefs, assumptions, values and norms, distinctive in important aspects of outlook and behaviour. They become a sub-culture.

The tolerant, pluralistic character of modern British society has disguised the extent to which it has become post-Christian, and the institutional legacy of British Christianity's traditional historical importance in national life has delayed and obscured the realization of seemingly inevitable sub-cultural status. But as Eric Treacy, Anglican Bishop of Wakefield, put it in 1974: 'The time is upon us when a man who involves himself with the Church, who practises his faith in the common ways of life – will do so against the conventions of society.' It was easy, even in the 1970s, to underestimate the progress of de-Christianization in Britain, Treacy argued. 'We are still living', he said,

on our capital of Christian inheritance. Today, there remain in our national attitudes, traditions and standards which are part of our Christian inheritance, but the capital is running out. The next generation will inherit less than we did in the way of Christian values.[1]

In examining, historically and sociologically, the processes through which Britain has become a post-Christian society, and the ways in which the British Churches have come to terms (or failed to come to terms) with their increasing marginality in that society, this book advances definite conclusions. It is interpretative as well as descriptive. It even makes certain predictions about likely future developments. Many British Christians may not like its conclusions about such things as secularization, ecumenism, theological liberalism or the likely emergence of a modern sectarian Christianity – but for Christians in a post-Christian world religious trends and realities are, presumably, bound to be unpalatable. An accurate picture, however unfavourable, is preferable to a false one, and sanguinity is no substitute for realism as a basis for pastoral planning, evangelistic strategy or the formation of organizational policy.

So the book is neutral in its spirit of inquiry and social-scientific in its approach. Its conclusions have grown out of a decade or so of research and writing about modern British religion, and especially out of a detailed acquaintance with patterns of church growth and organizational decline, and a continuing interest in relationships between religion and society. Inevitably, such processes of research and analysis involve an accumulation of scholarly debts. Ken Inglis and Robert Currie, good friends and shrewd critics both, have been consistently helpful, influential and deserving of immense gratitude. Murdith McLean, philosophical friend of this too-hasty historian, will not like many of the arguments which follow, but his hours of counsel have not been lost upon them, and none of them will, I hope, be thought to deprecate the art of listening for that 'still, small voice saying God is on the loose'. I am grateful also to friends and colleagues at the University of New South Wales for listening to chapter drafts and discussing troublesome arguments, and to the University itself for providing Study Leave to support the project.

ALAN D. GILBERT
*University of New South Wales.*

## NOTE

1.  *C. of E. Newspaper,* 29 March 1974.

# Introduction

'But it seems that something has happened that has never
    happened before: though we know not just when, or
    why, or how, or where.
Men have left GOD not for other gods, they say, but for
    no god; and this has never happened before.'

(T.S. Eliot, 'Choruses from *The Rock*')

During the summer of 1976, over a period of several weeks, *The Times*
published in its correspondence columns a somewhat bizzarre exchange
of letters on the problem of what to do with growing numbers of
redundant church-buildings. The debate focussed on the Church of
England, although not because redundancy is a peculiarly Anglican
problem. But in the Church of England alone, during the 1970s official
redundancies have been running at more than 100 per year, and for
some time the Save Britain's Heritage movement and kindred bodies
have been stepping up efforts to preserve the historical and architectual
legacy of what they clearly regard as a threatened component of British
culture. Indeed, under the aegis of a 1968 Pastoral Measure official
pastoral committees have been set up within the Church to ensure,
among other things, a rational and dignified disposal of material
resources justified no longer by public patronage. What should be done
with the empty churches, that is the question.

*The Times* published various ingenious suggestions, together with
some expressions of concern about current and threatened abuses of
once sacred premises. 'Gentle ruination', some writers suggested,
would produce fine historical monuments for the future. Others took a
more practical view. Marcus Binney, chairman of Save Britain's

Heritage, pointed out helpfully that 'Churches and chapels often have the high ceilings required for popular indoor sports such as badminton, five-a-side football, table tennis, boxing and gymnastics, not to mention basketball, cricket practice, fencing, hockey, netball, volleyball, wrestling and weight training.' Angry letters came from people offended by the sight of ecclesiastical-looking bingo halls, warehouses and private homes. And the possibility that 'a font where the sacred mystery of Christian baptism has been practised for generations should now grace someone's "chic" living room' appalled members of the Norfolk Churches Trust.[1]

But no-one suggested that the problem of redundancy might be eliminated or reduced, or that means might be found to fill empty churches with new generations of religious worshippers. There was a *post-mortem* air to the entire debate, and it was this that made *The Times's* correspondence columns, for a short time, a window into the contemporary religious scene in Britain. For perhaps the most devastating evidence of the decline of religion in the society is the way in which it is so often simply taken for granted that religiosity is an increasingly peripheral aspect of social activity and human consciousness. Numerous exceptions might be cited, of course – from instances of church growth and religious enthusiasm to the careful evaluations of scholars in sociology and theology suggesting that secularization is more illusory than real. Yet the 'conventional wisdom' about the role of religion in the modern world certainly is that religious convictions and religious influences are less pervasive and less important than they have been in the past, and that the decline is likely to continue.

The currency of this kind of thinking is of considerable importance, not least because 'conventional wisdom', however false or simplistic, has a tendency to become self-fulfilling prophecy, but also because the very notion of a *religionless* culture is so distinctively modern a phenomenon. Unbelief has an ancient pedigree, as indeed has religious apathy, but throughout history religion – like the poor – has been with the human species always. The possibility that an entire culture, not just elite elements within it, might dispense with religion altogether is uniquely a product of that modern Western civilization which (to compound its importance), is proving so exportable even in a post-colonial age. British society is just one of a variety of cultural milieux in which religion appears to be in crisis; and too many wise heads have decided, in Eliot's words, that something is happening in the modern world which 'has never happened before', for the 'conventional wisdom' to be dismissed out of hand.

Has what Dietrich Bonhoeffer called 'the religious *a priori* of man' been lost in the context of modern industrial society? Are we entering a 'post-Christian' phase of Western civilization? Such questions raise a whole cluster of problems, historical as well as theoretical. Historians, however, have in the past very largely conceded the study of secularization to sociologists and theologians, and despite the evident historical competence which many of these scholars have brought to their work, the historical dimension of the subject remains one of the least explored. This book is written in the belief that by examining the history of religion in modern Britain in the light of relevant social theory, it will be possible both to sharpen the focus of the specifically historical inquiry and at the same time evaluate aspects of the theory in terms of this actual historical example.

One reason why historical approaches to secularization remain under-developed is the traditional separation of 'religious' and 'secular' themes in historical studies. Even historians who have treated both themes have often been least confident in discussing *relationships* between the two. Yet it is in interactions between the 'Church' and the 'world' that the historian of secularization discovers his central theme. 'The salt of the earth', Jesus Christ called his followers, implying that their function would be to permeate society at large with the beliefs and values which he had taught. Yet Christianity was scarcely a generation old before St Paul had found reason to warn the young Church to 'separate' itself from a profane society. These were the two sides of the perennial dilemma of being the 'Church' in the 'world'. The goal remained to spread *godliness* throughout the world, but *worldliness* was something to be resisted and feared. The apostolic warning, echoed repeatedly as the centuries passed, recognized that the wider social and cultural environment of a religious culture has a profound and sometimes subversive influence on its development. And Christian history has illustrated in numerous ways that the cost to the Church of shaping the wider culture is to be itself shaped and re-shaped by a myriad of inescapable involvements.

The history of religion, in short, has never been an autonomous process. Religious consciousness, religious organizations and religious ideologies act and react upon their secular counterparts in complex ways. What follows, on the one hand, is that social and cultural history can ill-afford to ignore the so-called 'religious factor'; but equally, the evolution of religious beliefs and values is fully explicable only when placed alongside those wider developments which accompany and condition it. Such developments can include anything from changes in the material circumstances of life, in the nature of the human habitat or in human knowledge and mastery of the natural world, to changes in the role which 'secular consciousness is accorded by the *zeitgeist* of an age.

Any really comprehensive history of religion, it might be argued, must concentrate as fully on the 'world' as it does on the 'Church', but in a study of secularization there is an obvious sense in which the secular context must actually take priority in the analysis. It has been the modern British experience, for example, for Christian traditions to find themselves preoccupied increasingly with rearguard actions against social and cultural trends of an apparently hostile kind. Secular modes of thought and behaviour have had the initiative in the interaction between 'Church' and urban-industrial 'world'. This is not to imply that British Christianity has been a passive victim of forces external to itself, or that religious institutions, beliefs and organizations have varied automatically with the processes of secularization. Part Three of this study will in fact concentrate on the kinds of options which have been available to religious groups in the secularizing society, and on the ways in which different churches and church parties have responded to them. Yet the fact remains that the role of religion in modern British history has been not so much active as reactive.

Part Three's examination of religious responses to secularization can therefore be seen in consequential as well as sequential relationship to earlier sections of the Book. The theme of Part Two is the historical development in Britain of a secular 'world'. The primary historical context of modern British Christianity, it will argue, has been the emergence of an essentially *areligious* culture, and the growth of social structures, settlement patterns and life-styles hostile to the traditional social forms of British religion. The underlying question will be why this society, like other societies in the industrial world, should have become increasingly impermeable to the flow of religious ideas and the penetration of religious activities? Without answering such a question it is simply superficial to concentrate on reactions to secularization within the churches.

But if Parts Two and Three are intended to present an integrated historical analysis, Part One has been planned on the assumption that certain theoretical considerations must precede such an analysis. Secularization is a theme in which the historian cannot ignore relevant social theory, or proceed without reference to the debates of specialists in other disciplines. Nor should he wish to. The best modern history should be concerned to examine the nature of our contemporary society by explaining how it has emerged. It must explore processes of change and continuity with a sense of the future as well as the past. It must, in short, have a sociological dimension, even while it seeks to avoid merely imposing social theory on historical evidence. For the theoretical insights of other disciplines, so long as they are constantly evaluated and qualified in the light of historical evidence, often can add subtlety and precision to the historical method. In any case, so vague, varied and inconsistent are the ways in which concepts like 'religion' and 'secularization' are used, that only a systematic introduction of its relevant theoretical assumptions can insure that a history of secularization means the same to its readers as it does to its author.

## NOTE

1.  *The Times,* 15 August 1976.

# PART ONE

# Approaching the decline of religion in the modern world

'. . . whereas the basis of things amidst all chance and change has in Europe generally been for ever so long supernatural Christianity, and far more so in England than in Europe generally, this basis is certainly going – going amidst the full consciousness of the continentals that it is going, and amidst the provincial unconsciousness of the English that it is going.'

(Matthew Arnold, *Letters*)

# CHAPTER ONE

# Secularization and the historian

Without pre-judging any of the issues caught up in the idea of secularization, something that can be affirmed with confidence is the reality of a marked decline of churchgoing and church membership in twentieth-century Britain. The extent of this decline, and variations in its impact from area to area and denomination to denomination, will be examined in detail as the analysis proceeds. But that serious organizational and institutional decay has occurred is beyond question, and indeed this must rank as one of the most conspicuous changes in social habits in recent decades. But however conspicuous, it is also one of the most obscure and least understood of social processes, and there is profound and continuing disagreement about both the nature and the significance of the change. Has 'religion' really declined, or have the changes been confined to various external manifestations of an otherwise unabated religious impulse? And if there has been an actual decline of 'religion', what will be the long-term social and cultural consequences of the change? Need anyone who is neither an antiquarian nor a member of the churchgoing minority really attempt to understand the phenomenon?

Apparently not, judging from the general histories of modern Britain. Major contributions such as A. J. P. Taylor's *English History 1914–1945*, C. L. Mowat's *Britain Between the Wars*, W. N. Medlicott's *Contemporary England*, or even A. Marwick's *Britain in the Century of Total War*, for all its special attention to social aspects of the subject, have almost nothing to say about religion; and none suggests that the decline of religion need be adduced to explain anything sufficiently important to warrant inclusion in an overview of the twentieth century. As a *genre*, however, general history is deficient precisely at the point where the mainstream political, constitutional, economic, and cultural developments of an age interact with the more subterranean movements of popular consciousness and social behaviour which in the long run create the context determining the shape of major events. Religion – or more precisely, religion's decline – may in fact have been involved in the shaping of modern Britain to an extent still difficult to perceive.

Processes of cultural decline are not often newsworthy. Indeed, the intrusion of something new into a cultural system is likely to be much more noticeable than a process of decline, even when it is really far less significant. For, especially among those members of a society whose socialization has accustomed them from childhood to cope without the waning beliefs, values and institutions, negative cultural change often commands little attention. Yet if what is disappearing has been important in the past, its elimination will either reflect or require commensurate changes in other areas of social structure or cultural life. In the case of the decline of religion there is a significant body of sociological opinion endorsing the fears of moralists who see only demoralization and anomie, on the one hand, or new and perhaps sinister forms of institutional coercion on the other, as the alternatives facing a society bereft of a once-normative system of religious beliefs and practices. The great conservative, Edmund Burke, made much of such possibilities in his famous, hostile critique of the rational spirit which he saw underlying the French Revolution; and many of the eminent Victorians who agonized over the future of religion did so chiefly because they doubted seriously whether social order and morality could survive without it. It would be foolish simply to discount such fears.

Equally, however, closer examination may dispel the anxiety. British society may turn out to be adjusting quite adequately to a post-Christian situation; or alternatively, the closer scrutiny may reveal a surprising persistence of religion beneath fairly superficial institutional problems. For it is arguable that a widespread abandonment of churchgoing habits, however conspicuous as a social process, has relatively little to do with the currency of basic religious beliefs and values. Perhaps what is often described as 'secularization' represents a metamorphosis of religion rather than a decline. Religious commitment – taking new institutional forms, expressing ultimate truths through novel systems of theology, and possibly requiring little associational organization to sustain it – may be able to survive and flourish in a society which retains some church buildings for their historical value and converts others into theatres, concert halls, offices, warehouses or building-sites.

Certain new or exotic religious and quasi-religious phenomena have in fact become a feature of the kind of cultures which in the modern world seem to be stultifying traditional religious institutions. And some sociologists of religion, feeling that a general 'decline of religion' cannot be inferred from evidence of institutional difficulties, have made much of the continuing vitality of superstition in societies in Western Europe and the United States. Belief in ghosts and spirits, in astrology and various forms of divination, in the power of luck and the efficacy of manifold taboos, together with other forms of superstition, plays a continuing role in modern life, albeit an enigmatic one. So, in recent years, do numerous quasi-religious phenomena ranging from the quest for ultimate meaning through encounter groups, communes, affinity groups and other semi-ritualistic forms of social behaviour. Two things remain problematical, however: first, whether the elements of superstition in modern culture are anything other than residual traces of a declining religiosity; and secondly, whether the 'new gods' of ecstasy and group interaction are ever likely to appeal to anything other than a sub-cultural minority.

## RELIGION AND RELIGIOSITY

To begin to answer these questions is to enter a minefield of semantic confusion. If distinctions such as that between 'secular' and 'sacred' are even a little cloudy – if words like 'religion' or 'secularization' are used in even slightly divergent senses - the result can be empty, futile debate or (what may be worse) illusory consensus. Moreover, there are ways of understanding the concept of 'religion' which rule out most theories of secularization on purely analytical or logical grounds. Any definition which regards religiosity as an innate and therefore universal human impulse comes into this category, as does almost any definition which identifies as 'religious' phenomena lacking any supernatural orientation whatever. If religious faith is to be defined in terms of mankind's 'ultimate concerns' – to take an obvious example – then it can be threatened by nothing short of the extinction of the human species! Different things may concern men ultimately at different periods of human history, and particular organizational, ideological and devotional expressions of such concerns will wax and wane. But 'religion', so understood, cannot but persist in one form or another. It will change, but it cannot decline.

The same kind of point applies to all definitions which count as 'religious' any cultural phenomenon involving the use of ritual, the evocation of awe, or the ideological systematization of a worldview. There is not necessarily a supernatural element in any of these things. Hence such definitions of 'religion' can cover everything from orthodox Christianity to the so-called 'secular religions', including Marxism, Fascism, transcendental meditation, or even the ritualized hysteria of a Wembley Cup Final or a pop concert. To use 'religion' so inclusively is of doubtful value. Definitions are not in themselves either true or false, of course. They are merely more or less useful, within a particular context, than the available alternatives. But when they lump together things which are in important respects essentially dissimilar, loose definitions lead to unnecessarily vague description and unnecessarily imprecise analysis. The best definition, then, is one which is clear about what it includes and what it excludes, and useful in the sense that it elucidates genuine similarities and differences, actual continuities and discontinuities, within the relevant subject. In the case of 'religion', for example, there are obvious grounds for dissatisfaction with a definition which fails to make a distinction in kind between a football fan's devotion towards his team, however total and impassioned it might be, and a devout Christian's reverence for a transcendent God.

In this book 'religion' will be used to describe *any system of values, beliefs, norms, and related symbols and rituals, arising from attempts by individuals and social groups to effect certain ends, whether in this world or in any future world, by means wholly or partly supernatural*. In terms of such a definition, 'religious consciousness' describes an individual's awareness of, or belief in, the supernatural as an actually or potentially obtrusive factor in human existence; 'religious culture' describes any cultural system, or any element with a cultural system, shaped by religious consciousness; and religious organizations and institutions are those arising from social activities prompted wholly or partly by religious consciousness or religious culture. 'The supernatural' is of course a concept fraught with complexity in certain contexts, but its present denotation simply reflects common usage. Supernatural phenomena are manifestations of some agency above the forces of nature; they lie outside the ordinary or naturally predictable operation of cause and effect.

These definitions deliberately adopt an anthropological perspective. 'Religion' is a matter of human consciousness, human experience, human activity; or more specifically, it has to do with aspects of these things which involve human perceptions of a supernatural reality. Whether or not the supernatural actually exists is a separate issue, and undoubtedly a crucial one. This was the point of Carl Gustav Jung's insistence that as a psychologist he could speak of 'God' only as an archetype: as an image imprinted on the human psyche. 'The religious point of view puts the accent on the imprinter', he wrote in *Psychology and Alchemy*, 'Whereas scientific psychology emphasises the *typos*, the imprint, the only thing it can understand.'[1] This kind of distinction is equally relevant to the study of religion in all the social sciences, including social history, and it has important implications for the study of secularization.

The social scientist cannot argue validly, as Feuerbach's famous analysis led him to argue more than a century ago, that the supernatural is *nothing but* a figment of the human psyche, or that God is merely 'the highest subjectivity of man abstracted from himself. . . .'[2] But it is no less invalid to deduce the actual existence of God or supernature from the fact of human religiosity, as Jung perhaps wished to do in his enigmatic observation that 'an archetype presupposes a printer'.[3] According to Christian theology a spiritual world pre-dated the existence both of human beings and *ipso facto* of human religion, and its continued existence is presumably no less independent of the vagaries of human consciousness. To deduce the 'death of God' from the decline of religion, or the existence of the supernatural from evidence of human religiosity, is in either case to make a kind of metaphysical judgment for which sociology, history, or related disciplines have no criteria. So 'religion' is here defined in a way which limits the analysis to changing patterns of human consciousness, and to the social and cultural consequences of such changes.

Within these limits, however, the definition is intended to encompass within a single category the whole spectrum of human responses to the supernatural. In this sense it is an unusually inclusive definition, for it embraces as 'religious' what some sociologists and anthroplogists would call 'magic' or 'superstition'. The religion-magic distinction, while often illuminating, is extraordinarily difficult to sustain in a systematic analysis. Even in contemporary Britain, for example, for many evidently 'religious' people Christianity is interpreted as little more than an instrumentality placing them in touch with supernatural agencies. This may be regarded as a sub-Christian perception of supernatural reality, lacking the awe, reverence and submissiveness which the God of Christian theology warrants and demands, yet it counts, for present purposes, as a 'religious' position. For the object of the definition is not to capture the meaning of 'religion' as distilled by purist theology, but to denote what the term has meant to people who traditionally have regarded themselves as 'religious', and who have been so-regarded by their peers.

Purging popular religiosity of any trace of magico-superstitious elements would mean eliminating a whole host of beliefs and practices taken for granted by people considering themselves as orthodox as they are devout. Numerous examples might be cited. Traditional Catholic feelings about the actual, as distinct from symbolic, instrumentality of St Christopher medals, like habits (not uncommon among certain Evangelicals) of seeking divine guidance through a random, pin-pricking approach to Biblical texts, and like the still-widespread notion that religiosity *per se* facilitates success in business, study, sport or family life, could not, on a rigorous religion-magic distinction, be allocated automatically to the former category. Yet these things unquestionably are part of the religious-cultural heritage whose decline is the subject of this study.

What follows is that any satisfactory analysis of secularization must range broader and deeper than the iceberg tip of strictly orthodox theologies and responses, and include all aspects of 'the cultic milieu'[4] which are shaped by human perceptions of the supernatural. But because many of the subterranean theologies and deviant cults have a derivative and dependent relationship to an established religious-cultural orthodoxy, there is a danger of over-estimating their importance in a secularizing society. Granted that the essence of 'religion' is a supernatural orientation of one kind or another, they must be included; but what they signify about the relationship between religion and society must remain one of the central problems in the study of secularization.

Other popular cultic phenomena, however, can only be regarded as 'religious' at the cost of analytical precision and (in an historical study) consistency of usage. The present definition is therefore intended to distinguish clearly between what is 'religious' and what – in recognition of its ambiguous character – is sometimes referred to as a 'functional equivalent of religion', a 'religious surrogate', or a 'quasi-religious' phenomenon. It is, in short, a definition which emphasises the discontinuity between 'religion' and the kinds of 'secular religions' referred to earlier. The point is that while things like Marxism, transcendental meditation, hallucinatory drugs, or spectator sport – each in a different way – sometimes operate in modern societies, as religion more commonly operated in the past, as sources of social cohesion, foci for personal or group identity, or modes of interpreting or coming to terms with life, it does not follow that these things and religiosity are indistinguishable. Social cohesion can be buttressed in many different ways, and individual worldviews are sometimes fashioned out of beliefs and assumptions which neither involve the supernatural nor evoke numinosity. To require the term 'religion' to include all such responses is to define it so vaguely as to rob it of considerable analytical value.

In an historical study, moreover, there is the question of traditionally accepted usage to be considered, and this is especially pertinent when it is the decline of 'religion' which is under scrutiny. Obviously, if the traditional understanding of what counts as 'religion', and what does not, has excluded varieties of belief and behaviour now considered as 'religious' or 'quasi-religious', the effect will be to obscure the full extent of the decline. To take an extreme example, it might be possible to obviate the need to speak of the decline of religion in Britain by calling the motor car, the television set, the pop idol or the sporting hero the 'new gods' of the modern era, but to do so would be to obscure an immense discontinuity in the social history of the society. For these things have little or nothing in common with the religious traditions of the past, except perhaps in certain of the latent functions which they perform. Some scholars have conceded as much by use of the term 'religious surrogates' to describe the 'new gods'. But the increasing vogue of a 'surrogate' is perhaps more likely to be evidence of the decline of the genuine article than evidence of its persistence.

So the insistence that genuine religiosity presupposes some kind of supernatural orientation rests on the precision and historical consistency which the definition affords. It clarifies fundamental processes of cultural change in Western civilization where more inclusive definitions only obfuscate them. For Matthew Arnold was right when he wrote in 1882 that 'supernatural Christianity' had 'for ever so long' provided 'the basis of things amidst all chance and change' in Europe. It remains for the historian of secularization to decide whether he was also right in observing that by the late Victorian era this basis was 'certainly going – going amidst the full consciousness of the continentals that it is going, and amidst the provincial unconsciousness of the English that it is going'.[5]

And whether Arnold was right or wrong in this judgment, there can be little doubt about the critical influence which certain forms of supernaturalism have played in shaping human consciousness and human culture. The presence or absence of belief in supernatural forces – the question of whether these beliefs are pervasive and influential rather than peripheral and unimportant – is among the most fundamental criteria of cultural differentiation and cultural change. Nor is this just a commonsense viewpoint. For at least since Max Weber's emphasis on the pervasive social, intellectual and technological consequences of what he called 'the disenchantment of the world', the resort to means wholly or partly supernatural to explain or manipulate the environment, or on the other hand the rejection of such means, have been recognized widely as basic alternatives in the fashioning of cultural systems.

## THE SECULARIZATION PROCESS

The chosen definition of 'religion' thus implies a clear distinction between 'religious' and 'secular' modes of thought and activity, and in so doing offers an intelligible view of the related concept of 'secularization'. In the 'secular' mode the world is conceived in terms of natural causation, interpreted in a matter-of-fact, objective way, and regarded as manipulable through physical agencies, human institutions and empirical logic. But viewed in 'religious' terms it remains a place of mystery, caught up in a supernatural order which is extra-empirical, arbitrary and personal, and which is open to human influence and manipulation only – if at all – through ritual, magic or religion. Obviously these are merely contrast-concepts. No individual worldview or cultural system ever has been entirely 'religious' or entirely 'secular' in these terms. Nevertheless, there is no clearer way of analysing secularization than that which sees it essentially as a gradual intrusion of 'secular' consciousness into areas of thought and activity dominated previously by 'religious' perceptions of reality.

A thoroughly secular culture would be one in which norms, values, and modes of interpreting reality, together with the symbols and rituals which express and reinforce them, have been emancipated entirely from assumptions of human dependence on supernatural agencies or influences. In it the natural world would be regarded as autonomous, and knowledge, values and social structures would be ordered upon purely mundane principles. 'Secularization' describes the social and cultural processes tending to produce such a secular milieu. It includes, historically, all those developments and influences within any society which have been antithetical towards 'religious' assumptions, values, practices and institutions; and where successful, its effect has been gradually to transform more or less religious cultures into increasingly secular ones.

Such generalizations beg a basic question about the nature of human consciousness, for it is one thing to describe in theoretical terms what secularization involves, but quite another to explain why, and under

9

what conditions, it occurs. What is the relationship between 'religious' and 'secular' modes of thought, and by what logic – through what mechanisms of psychological or cultural change – does the 'secular' encroach upon the 'religious'? No theory of secularization can successfully avoid this issue. For there can be no explanation of the decline of religion which does not at least imply some sort of answer to the question why religion exists in the first place. Most obviously, perhaps, any linear theory of secularization which implies an essentially one-directional movement of history away from predominantly 'religious' types of culture and towards predominantly 'secular' ones, presupposes some quite fundamental link between secularization and what sometimes is called *modernization*.

The contrast between the highly pervasive role of religion in so-called 'primitive' societies and the comparatively limited influence which it appears to exercise in modern industrial societies today, may perhaps provide evidence of an overall movement of human history and culture in a secular direction. But whether or not it can be so-regarded, it certainly provides a clue to the kinds of conditions under which secularization occurs. In 'primitive' cultures, however irrelevant the religious-secular distinction for the actual participants, it is safe to say that no sphere of thought or activity is free from 'religious' assumptions. Religion is *cognitively* significant in the sense that natural phenomena are explained partly with reference to supernatural forces; it is important *instrumentally* in the sense that people rely on such forces to help them control the natural order, or manipulate it, whether to procure bounty in harvest, victory in war, recovery from illness, or protection against the manifold dangers of an unpredictable world; and it has a basic *expressive* significance, offering the only widely-satisfying means of symbolizing and legitimating the hopes, fears and aspirations of individuals.

This is what Weber called an 'enchanted garden' world. So ubiquitous are the 'breaking-points' in human perceptions of reality – the points at which natural, empirical, mundane explanations fail to cope with human experience – that all aspects of life seem to involve supernatural, capricious forces and therefore to evoke 'religious' responses. But in a modern cultural context the 'garden' has become radically 'disenchanted', even for people who remain deeply religious. For the latter the expressive significance of religion may be unaffected or even heightened, and in many cases the supernatural is still conceded a vital instrumental role *for a future world,* but for all participants in a modern culture modes of understanding and manipulating the *present world* have been largely secularized. The natural order has acquired a substantial measure of autonomy from the supernatural; and in contrast with 'primitive' cultures, the residuum to which religion provides answers and dictates responses no longer covers vast areas and all aspects of human consciousness.

Words like 'breaking-points' and 'residuum' imply a 'gaps' theory of religiosity, and the implication is deliberate. For this is the key to understanding the intrusion of 'secular' consciousness into areas of thought and activity shaped previously by religion. 'In every religion', wrote the German theologian, Albrecht Ritschl, 'what is sought with the help of the superhuman power reverenced by man is a solution of the contradiction in which man finds himself as both part of nature and a spiritual personality claiming to dominate nature.'[6] Human beings have shown a propensity for religious behaviour – a propensity which sub-human species evidently lack – because they respond to the world consciously and reflectively, not just instinctively, and because they can transcend their physical immersion in the natural order and regard themselves in objective terms. As a result they face questions about meaning, significance and morality in life, and aspire to know, to understand, and at least in a measure to control their environment and their destiny. But these selfsame faculties which give a cosmic dimension to human consciousness also induce awareness of the constraints which nature imposes, of mankind's relative ignorance and powerlessness, and of the seeming brevity and triviality of mundane existence. It is in this tension between consciousness and creatureliness, between 'flesh' and 'spirit', that human religiosity has its roots.

The Semetic allegory of the Garden of Eden makes an ancient and arresting statement of this position: the temptation to be godlike is as old as the human race, but the fruit of the Tree of Knowledge is the realization that mankind is vulnerable and limited. Consciousness thus carries with it a sense of the infinite while self-consciousness brings awareness of an inescapable finitude, and the result is a profound human hunger for some kind of transcendent knowledge, power and authority to bridge the gap between attainment and aspiration. Religiosity has been the most significant human response to this situation, obtruding into human consciousness as people turn to the supernatural to find salvation from the numerous consequences of their essentially human failure to be godlike. It provides answers to questions otherwise unanswerable, it promises power where human knowledge and technical skill can do no more, it offers hope beyond human optimism, certainty beyond human powers of prediction, life (in some cases) beyond physical death.

But while this is an impressive catalogue of junctions, the view of human religiosity underlying it provides clearly for a plausible theory of secularization. For however carefully theological rationalizations are constructed to resist the conclusion, religious consciousness has always been concerned primarily with those cognitive, practical and emotional areas of human experience in which natural, matter-of-fact, this-worldly responses and solutions have proved partly or totally unsatisfactory. The very concept of 'salvation', so central to all religious traditions in one form or another, implies as much. Even in the most profoundly religious cultures, in short, religion is a final resort, or an ancillary response, rather than a first option in human attempts to interpret and influence physical, social and psychological events and experiences. That is to say, where there has been a non-religious way of explaining or influencing such events and experiences the human inclination generally has been to welcome it. Thus in a very important sense the vogue of 'religious' consciousness depends on the scope and significance of that residuum of human experience which appears neither explicable, predictable nor meaningful in natural, mundane terms.

Conversely, secularization occurs as this residuum diminishes. Limits to human knowledge, to the power at mankind's disposal, and to the predictability of the world, have not remained stationary. The 'breaking-points' in 'secular' consciousness have varied accordingly, and with them have changed the circumstances under which people have turned to the supernatural for assurance and assistance. Perhaps the best-known analysis linking this kind of 'gaps' theory of religion with the secularization process is in Dietrich Bonhoeffer's famous prison correspondence, in which 'a growing tendency to assert the autonomy of man and the world' is seen as characteristic of the devolution of modern culture. Indeed, what made these letters so stimulating for later theologians was Bonhoeffer's courage in facing the possibility that religiosity might prove to have been 'an historical and temporary form of human self-expression'. Religion might not always remain 'a condition of salvation', he wrote,

> for Religious people speak of God when human perception is (often just from laziness) at an end, or human resources fail: it is really always the *Deus ex machina* they call to their aid, either for the so-called solving of insoluble problems or as a support in human failure – always, that is to say, helping out human weakness or on the borders of human existence. Of necessity, that can only go on until men can, by their own strength, push those borders a little further, so that God becomes superfluous as a *Deus ex machina*.[7]

Bonhoeffer almost certainly exaggerated the present autonomy of man and the world. Awareness of the 'borders of human existence' has not disappeared, even in the most developed of modern cultures, and indeed it has shown signs of increasing in recent years as serious global problems of resource scarcity and environmental pollution have impinged more and more strongly upon public consciousness in industrialized societies. Moreover, in all such societies there remain sufficient grim reminders of human powerlessness and failure to induce traditional religious responses to the quest for salvation from life's dangers, uncertainties and transience. Yet while there is no imminent prospect of a society thoroughly secular, the fact remains that as an *historical model* Bonhoeffer's understanding of the impact of secularization seems entirely justified. For if 'secular' modes of thought tend to become normative whenever they offer plausible and practical ways of understanding the world, then any growth of human technical skill or empirical knowledge, any innovation in economic organization or social structure tending to mitigate poverty, suffering or insecurity, or any humanistic development in metaphysics or the expressive arts, is *prima facie* likely to create a cultural context antithetical to 'religious' consciousness. And by the same logic, of course, the model could allow us to make sense of cultural changes involving a revival of 'religious' consciousness in areas of thought once secularized. For this is a theory of secularization which in no sense implies that the making of a 'post-Christian' society need be an irreversible process.

In this context it may be worth stressing that it is not the validity of a 'religious' worldview, but its relevance, that is challenged by such a process. In discussing the definition of 'religion' care has been taken to separate human religiosity from questions about the objective reality of the supernatural. Social, cultural or material changes in the direction of what might loosely be termed 'modernization' do not, logically, make religiosity any less viable than it has been in the past; but they *do* tend to create a situation in which it becomes increasingly possible to construct coherent worldviews without resort to 'religious' hypotheses. Such worldviews may be less comprehensive than those they have replaced, for their utility is restricted largely to making sense of mundane, this-worldly existence; but this apparent disadvantage seems to be balanced by the fact that the enhanced mastery over nature, and the increased material comfort and security that have gone hand-in-hand with modernization, have guaranteed a human preoccupation with the present life and the temporal world.

Thus the modern mind does not have new, 'secular' answers to all the questions which challenged earlier generations – only to some of them. The other questions it has largely ceased to ask, and perhaps even to understand. It is noteworthy that Max Weber, the twentieth

13

century's most outstanding student of the modernization, could say of himself: 'I am a-musical as far as religion is concerned, and have neither the desire nor the capacity to build religious architectures in myself.'[8] He saw that the cultural concomitants of modernization – the 'rationalization' and 'disenchantment' of the world – involved an almost inescapable narrowing of human consciousness. The triumph of scientific, empirical, rational values in Western thought had brought immense material and intellectual benefits, he knew, but as a result of their triumph other values were being lost. Autonomy seemed likely to be a very lonely prospect. 'Not summer's bloom lies ahead of us', he wrote in uncharacteristically moving vein, 'but rather a polar night of icy darkness and hardness'.[9]

Such was 'the fate of the times', and for persons unable or unwilling to bear it manfully Weber recommended traditional religiosity. But to him this seemed an evasion. For better or for worse, he believed, secularization had been an integral part of the making of modern Western culture. Modern minds could not therefore escape its consequences. Maybe this was an extreme view, but it is a salient fact that the crisis of contemporary Christianity lies not in challenges to the truth of its dogmas, but in the fact that (like Weber himself) people in a secular culture have become increasingly 'tone-deaf' to any orchestration of those dogmas. A secular culture, in short, is an environment in which the very *a priori* plausibility of a religious worldview is at stake, and it is with the development of this crisis of plausibility that a history of secularization must be chiefly concerned.

## THE BRITISH EXAMPLE

The following chapters are concerned primarily with the history of secularization in modern Britain, and their object is not so much to advance some general theory of secularization by using a British example, as to advance the historical study of modern British culture by investigating the apparent decline of religion as a force on the life of that culture. Yet the fact remains that the decline of religion is not a peculiarly British phenomenon. Throughout most of history, while the religiosity of mankind has been expressed in various ways from culture to culture, an underlying religious impulse has been more or less universal; and in a similar way, secularization, although varying in pace and in specific social and institutional manifestations, appears to involve common psychological and cultural characteristics whenever and wherever it occurs. So there is a sense in which what follows is a case-study of a particular understanding of secularization: one based on the kind of 'gaps' theory of religiosity outlined earlier in this chapter. As such, it is bound to have certain implications for comparable cultural contexts in other societies.

An historical model of secularization derived from the 'gaps' theory does appear to fit very well the *prima facie* evidence that the decline of religion has accelerated rapidly in the industrial age. In Britain, about two centuries ago, vast economic enterprise and technological ingenuity gave birth to the world's first Industrial Revolution, a breakthrough which many nations have since sought to emulate. The result has been a change in the environment of human life so immense that few aspects, if any, of social organization, cultural reality or human consciousness have escaped profound metamorphosis wherever industrialization has triumphed. And the direction of the change undoubtedly has been towards the realization – however illusory – of 'the autonomy of man and the world'.

Thus to the extent that this book has a particular thesis, its theme is the relationship in modern Britain between the decline of religion and the emergence of a complex urban-industrial society. And for the purposes of such a theme, 'religion' still means 'Christianity' in the British context. Until very recently virtually all British religion has been essentially Christian in origin and ideology, but in the past two decades culturally-exotic religions have been introduced on a large scale by non-Christian immigrants. A survey of contemporary British religious behaviour would be incomplete without the inclusion of Muslims, Buddhists, and Sikhs, to name only the most obvious examples. Yet in a study of secularization they can have only a marginal relevance, for the essence of such a study is change over time in the role of religion in a society. Only if and when these immigrant groups have become integrated sufficiently into the mainstream culture to experience the social and ideological pressures affecting British Christianity in the industrial age, will the new religions – like the old – become testing-grounds for hypotheses about secularization. So it is to the predicament of contemporary British Christianity that the discussion now turns.

## NOTES

(Full bibliographical details are in the References on pp. 162–8.)
1.  Jung, C. G. (1953), p. 12.

2. Feuerbach, L. (1854), pp. 12-13.
3. Jung, C. G. (1953), p. 12.
4. A concept elaborated by Campbell, C. (1972), p. 122.
5. Arnold, M. (1895), p. 201.
6. Quoted by Niebuhr, R. (1941), p. 190.
7. Bonhoeffer, D. (1953), p. 124.
8. Quoted by Hughes, H. S. (1959), p. 315.
9. Gerth, H. H. and Mills, C. Wright (1946), p. 128.

# CHAPTER TWO

# Secularization and western culture

The making of post-Christian Britain has been part of a prolonged historical process. It represents the culmination, in Britain, of a slow, uneven transformation involving European civilisation as a whole. During the past two centuries industrialization has acted as a powerful catalyst to hasten the transformation. But the secularization process itself can be traced back to the formative stages of modern western culture: to that critical period between the Renaissance and the Enlightenment, and beyond it to the origins of the Judaeo-Christian tradition itself. While limitations of space and knowledge necessarily preclude any detailed historical analysis of so extended a period, an historical overview remains perhaps the most effective way of drawing attention to the kinds of continuities and changes linking traditional cultural milieux, where religious consciousness was powerful and pervasive, with the contemporary post-Christian situation in a society such as Britain. Moreover, to couch such an overview in terms of a chosen theoretical framework, such as that elaborated in Chapter One, is possibly the best way to prepare for more detailed analysis, in later chapters, of the modern industrial phase of secularization.

## THE ORIGINS OF SECULARIZATION

The seeds of secularization were implanted at the very genesis of the Judaeo-Christian tradition. Christianity inherited the radical theological and cosmological insights of an ancient Semitic people, a people, with the grand yet precarious vision of a monotheistic universe. Monotheism was a potent, creative cultural force, but its impact on religious consciousness was two-sided. The sublime religiosity it produced, enriched first Hebrew and later Christian consciousness; but by setting up a dichotomy between 'sacred' and 'profane' aspects of reality it established an intellectual framework within which secularization was almost bound to occur. A dialectical tension between 'religious' and 'secular' modes of thought became a fundamental of Judaism and, through it, of Christianity.

For in discovering the transcendent majesty of Yahweh – in accepting Him alone as truly divine – the Hebrews gained the power gradually to extricate themselves from the hegemony of 'false gods' and the mystifications of paganism. The natural world, a product of divine creativity but not itself divine, could now be regarded in mundane, matter-of-fact terms. Yahweh might from time to time intervene 'miraculously' to disturb its natural order, but any such instances of supernatural activity were to be regarded as aberrations in otherwise natural and (theoretically) predictable sequences of events. In this way, under the transcendental theology of monotheism, a rational 'religious' – 'secular' distinction began to take shape; and as the Second Commandment quite plainly stated, reverence or worship came to be regarded in Judaism idolatrous responses to any natural object or phenomenon. Such things were 'sacred' no longer.

Distinguishing between the Creator and the creation made possible a definite heightening of human religious consciousness. But it also set the stage for an eventual rationalization and disenchantment of the world. By clearly delineating a category of things not 'sacred', Judaism had created a context for 'secular' ideas and modes of inquiry to develop: a context which could expand to include everything explicable in natural, mundane terms. Nor did such secularizing tendencies lie entirely dormant during the Jewish era. For as Hellenic philosophical and scientific notions intruded into the Jewish world of the pre-Christian era, 'secular' elements became increasingly evident in Jewish culture. And wherever this cultural synthesis occurred, the rationalizing implications of monotheism left the residual polytheism of Hellenic culture with very little 'religious' plausibility indeed.

The Christian Church was heir to both the Jewish and the Greco-Roman worlds. If the former left it with a cognitive framework within which a substantial 'autonomy of man and the world' might evolve, the latter provided it with memories, long forgotten but never entirely lost, of a classical culture already partly secularized. For by the early Christian era, most of the elements of modern secular consciousness existed already, at least in embryo, in the literature, philosophy and art of Hellenic and Roman civilisation. It is true that the early Church was at odds with many aspects of this dominant culture, yet as Christianity evolved from the role of persecuted sect to the influential position of a state religion, it inevitably absorbed much of the spirit and content of classical culture. The old dialectical tension between 'religious' and 'secular' consciousness was thus internalized by the new religion of the west.

In the process, however, many of the most pronounced secularizing tendencies carried over from the ancient world were either eliminated or suppressed. The dialectic could work in two directions, not one. If secularization could occur, it could also be reversed; and during more than a millenium of Christian history this is exactly what happened. The history of the west from the collapse of Rome to the fall of Constantinople involved, in the famous words of Edward Gibbon, 'the triumph of barbarism and religion'. The perjorative tone may be unwarranted, but the fact was that medieval Christendom was a far more 'religious' culture than that which had been fashioned by Imperial Rome. After the Roman Empire had disintegrated, secularization had not simply been retarded, it had been effectively reversed.

The medieval world may have been a far cry from the 'enchanted garden' consciousness of primitive societies, but it certainly bore the marks of partial 're-enchantment'. In Weber's less than euphonious expression, it had been 're-sacralized'. The Catholic Church, in the centuries after the collapse of Rome, gradually established with its European 'world' a relationship allowing only minimal scope for 'secular' interpretations of reality. During the period from the ninth to the thirteenth centuries it assumed a paramount and pervasive role in the institutional life of Western Europe, providing Christianity with a physical and social *proximity* to its European constituency which was, and remains, unequalled. At the same time, in the intellectual, moral and aesthetic consciousness of medieval man, 'religious' values and assumptions regained the kind of normative influence which they had lost among some of the cultural elites of the classical world. A remarkable *congruity* was established between Christian theology and the dominant beliefs and values of the wider society. And at all levels of social life and human need the Christian religion acquired immense and ubiquitous *utility* in the minds of medieval men. At the level of popular consciousness, for example, it functioned as 'a vast reservoir of magical power, capable of being deployed for a variety of secular purposes'.[1]

In the 're-enchantment' and 're-sacralization' that went hand-in-hand with the Christianization of Europe, the scope and importance of 'secular' modes of thought had been curtailed significantly. As the term 'Christendom' implies, medieval culture was essentially religious, and medieval Europe owed its coherence to the common bonds of a basic Christian consensus. Yet within Christendom, buried under the weight of medieval religiosity, were hidden the seeds of a future, highly secularized Europe. And under the influence of the Renaissance the seeds began to germinate.

## THE LEGACY OF THE RENAISSANCE

After showing distinct symptoms of metamorphosis throughout the fourteenth century, the medieval 'Age of Belief' gave way in the fifteenth century to a new 'Age of Adventure'.[2] Europe experienced the 'Renaissance'. Use of the term should not be taken to imply that the preceding medieval period was one of cultural immobility, or that the transformation of European civilization in the fifteenth and sixteenth centuries occurred in the same way and for identical reasons from area to area. But it does imply the appearance of a major watershed in European history. And whatever its validity as a general historical concept, the idea of the Renaissance certainly illuminates the history of cultural secularization in Europe.

Not for some centuries after the Renaissance would the secularizing tendencies then released into western culture emerge as a direct, open threat to the Christian consensus which had undergirded European civilisation since the Carolingian age. But the 're-enchantment' of the medieval world – the 're-sacralization' of culture which had shaped medieval Christendom – was halted. Europeans began to examine their contemporary culture in terms increasingly critical, and to seek its enrichment through philosophical systems and intellectual perspectives salvaged from a classical world considerably more secular than their own. While overtly counter-religious idelogies had to await the Enlightenment of the late seventeenth century, the Renaissance set in train cultural and institutional processes which prepared Europe for the coming Enlightenment crisis.

One such process was the rise of a humanist tradition destined, in the long run, to play a dominant role in western civilization. Humanism was born out of subtle changes in the social and material circumstances of medieval life. Medieval Christendom had established an enviable congruity with a Europe essentially agrarian and feudal. That was its world: a world in which a more or less static economy had offered few opportunities for human initiative and improvement, at least for the vast majority of the population, and in which it had been simply unrealistic for men to place too high a value on this-worldly effort and success. But Renaissance thought blossomed in the outposts of a new kind of Europe. In the commercial cities of late-medieval Italy, and among the artists and intellectuals who found patrons there, in the thriving burgher communities of the Low Countries and the Rhine Valley, and in the urban cantons of the Swiss Confederacy, feudal values and expectations gave way to an outlook increasingly capitalistic. A way of life developed in which, for a significant proportion of the population, rational this-worldy initiative and endeavour promised rich rewards.

Humanism was a philosophical expression of this new, self-confident, inquisitive mentality. Initially it generated neither heresy nor irreligion – and such things could, in any case, have been dealt with more or less peremptorily by Catholic authorities in Church and State. Yet the equilibrium of medieval culture was disturbed by it. The medieval worldview had been highly spiritualized, highly abstract, and the human condition had seemed more acceptable when viewed as a temporary adjunct to more fundamental, eternal realities. But without disputing the primacy of the spiritual realm, the early humanists took specifically this-worldly phenomena with a new seriousness. The natural order was conceded an intrinsic importance. It was seen to manifest the glory of a Creator who took pleasure in human activities both within the creation and as part of it.

'Do not believe, my friend,' wrote Coluccio Salutati, the Florentine humanist, at the close of the fourteenth century, 'that to flee the crowd, to avoid the sight of beautiful things, to shut oneself up in a cloister, is the way to perfection. In fleeing from the world you may topple down from heaven to earth, whereas I, remaining among earthly things, shall be able to lift my heart securely up to heaven. In striving and working, in caring for your family, your friends, your city which comprises all, you cannot but follow the right way to please God'.[3] It was a statement which summed up perfectly the spirit of Renaissance humanism.

This was a far cry from the eighteenth-century presumption that 'The proper study of mankind is man', but it also represented an important break with the medieval past. The Christian consensus remained unquestioned, but there was a growing acceptance of rational criticism and free inquiry in areas where medieval consciousness had been constrained by dogmatic principle. Christian humanists became increasingly critical of anachronistic ecclesiastical forms and clerical abuses, and in their emphasis on individual Christian responsibility, and their willingness to countenance reasoned criticism of dogmatic authority (such as in Erasmus's scholarly detection of error in the previously-sacrosanct Vulgate), they created a climate where even more radical critiques might take root. The critical, humanistic spirit which they brought into European culture certainly could not be expected to ignore forever the kinds of ideas, attitudes and cognitive methods which pointed beyond the margins, not just of medieval scholasticism, but of the Catholic faith itself, and perhaps even of the Christian religion.

A second legacy of the Renaissance era was the emergence of science as a European cultural activity. It is a reflection of the extent to which a scientific ethos dominates modern western societies that we find it hard to realize that empirical science is not an inevitable aspect of intellectual culture. Yet it is a fact. Medieval learning, for example, was virtually devoid of genuine scientific curiosity, even after the rediscovery of Aristotelian scientific texts in the thirteenth century. Only in the sixteenth century, as this classical legacy was metamorphosed under the impact of humanist thought, did a modern scientific culture begin to take shape. The details of its emergence and prodigious growth are scarcely relevant to the present study, but the significance of the 'scientific revolution' as a potential source of secularization does require some elaboration.

Science had flourished in ancient Greece, where considerable progress had been made in the fields of medicine, physics, biology, mathematics and astronomy. But the Neoplatonism of the Roman era, with its rejection of empirical observation as a cognitive method – with its dependence on analogical reasoning – had already gone far towards stultifying the scientific spirit when the Christianization of European culture began. The influence of the Christian Fathers made little of empirical observation, and rejected the serious study of natural phenomena in favour of systematic theology. As the great Augustine put it, 'to seek out the hidden powers of nature' was a 'perverted aim'. The Christian philosopher, he taught, should 'rest content to be ignorant of the mysteries of the heavens and the earth'.[4] Such views prevailed in Europe, and were not effectively challenged, until the Renaissance.

The scientific revolution gave impetus to secularization not because it was anti-religious, but because it re-drew the distinction between 'religious' and 'secular' knowledge which the twin influences of Platonic and Christian thought had obscured. Medieval man had accepted a worldview in which natural phenomena were regarded as secondary and derivative aspects of more fundamental realities which were idealistic and spiritual. The thirteenth-century rediscovery of Aristotelian science had made little difference to this basic attitude precisely because under the influence of Scholasticism Aristotelianism had been subtly integrated into a comprehensive theological system. As Francis Bacon pointed out in 1605, by subjecting scientific speculation to theological constraints the Schoolmen had made scientific inquiry both difficult and 'perilous'.[5] For a scientific culture to develop, European intellectuals would have to accept the autonomy of the natural world as an arena for empirical investigation and 'secular' understanding.

Such a view emerged slowly, abetted by the critical, humanistic values of the Renaissance, but not without the kind of bitter controversy exemplified in Galileo's confrontation with religious authorities seeking to outlaw, on *a priori* theological grounds, a scientific theory based on the observation of nature. By the seventeenth century, however, the growth of a European scientific culture had become virtually irreversible. Up to the Enlightenment, and indeed beyond it, nearly all the scientists professed to be devout Christians. Many claimed to be motivated chiefly by the desire to understand God's handiwork in nature. But whatever their motives or their values, their work contributed to the secularization of the European 'world' in at least two ways.

In the first place, the advancement of science cultivated a field of human awareness in which 'religious' consciousness was epistemologically irrelevant. In 1327 Marsiglio of Padua had been declared a heretic for suggesting that nature and supernature were so separate that something which was false in one could be perfectly true in the other. The medieval world had been unready to accept that the world of nature might have such autonomy. But by the end of the Renaissance era this idea was insinuating itself deep into European culture. Bacon, for example, could write of the natural world that: 'in this theatre of man's life it is reserved only for God and angels to be lookers on'.[6] Science did not contradict religious faith, but neither was it dependent upon such faith. Moreover, its growth contributed to the secularization of European culture through the content, not just the mode, of scientific discovery.

The formulation and verification of scientific hypotheses in fields like medicine, chemistry, physics and astronomy, and even horticulture and animal husbandry, gradually constructed a 'secular' framework for interpreting aspects of human experience explicable earlier only with reference to supernatural, magico-religious agencies. The scientist might merely be describing the mechanics of a divinely-created universe, but the fact remained that he was doing so in meticulously practical, this-worldly terms. For although the heavens – and the earth, for that matter – were still seen to declare the glory of God, it was a necessary assumption of the scientific community that both proceeded from day to day according to natural, theoretically-predictable sequences of cause and effect. The scientific revolution, in short, gradually reduced religion's *instrumental* and *cognitive* utility in the present world; and this secularizing effect operated irrespective of the fact that in their discovery of nature many scientists found (as many continue to find), an inspiration which enhanced the *expressive* aspect of religious faith.

While scientists thus asserted the autonomy of nature from 'religious' modes of thought, Renaissance political philosophers made the same kind of point in the even more contentious area of political and social theory. Marsiglio's early fourteenth-century anticipation of Renaissance humanism, for example, had been concerned primarily with the nature of civil society. Medieval statecraft had brooked no distinction between 'the Christian' and 'the natural man'. Transformed through the mystery of Christian baptism, the natural man had become a partaker of spiritual qualities, obligations and responsibilities. An entire social order comprised of such men had, *ipso facto*, to be governed essentially by principles spiritually derived and legitimated. Thus, in Christendom, being a citizen had meant being a Christian, and excommunication from the Church had meant expulsion from civil society. The Church had wielded 'two swords' – a temporal as well as a specifically spiritual authority – and if Catholicism was an integral part of the State, so was religiosity an integral part of individual citizenship.

The secularization of political authority in Europe was to be a prolonged, and often traumatic process. Even when 'Enlightened' seventeenth-century rulers abandoned the 'divine right' theory in favour of rationalistic legitimations of political sovereignty, rudiments of the older, sacred conceptions continued to flourish – as indeed they flourish today, for example, in the role of religious functionaries in some of the rituals of the British constitutional system. But as the word 'rudiments' implies, the trend has long been towards the secularization of political ideology and social theory.

The process began with the first stirrings of Renaissance thought. Marsiglio, in 1343 declared by Pope Clement VI to be 'the worst ever of the heretics', spoke too early to enjoy the relative intellectual freedom of the Renaissance age, but his suggestion that it was man's humanity, not his Christianity, which should determine his social and political needs, was never effectively suppressed. 'Life in the next world, Marsiglio said, may be quite important, but the citizens as citizens were not concerned with it. For the function of the laws was to provide "good living" in this life and world . . . '.[7] In these words Walter Ullmann has summarized the underlying assumption of Marsiglio's radicalism. A century before Europe was exposed to the more fully developed, more thoroughly amoral political theories of Machiavelli, a basis had been laid for the gradual emancipation of the social order from the temporal authority and moral guardianship of the 'Church' over the 'world'. The trend, at least, pointed to the secular politics and 'scientific' social disciplines of the modern world.

Yet it was not simply intellectual ferment which made the Renaissance a crucial period in the history of European culture. Equally important were profound material and social changes which so transformed the human context as to give Renaissance intellectual activity its immense significance. Note has already been taken of the rise of new urban-commercial wealth, and of the associated changes in lifestyle which subtly undermined the more or less static models of economic enterprise and social reality around which medieval consciousness had formed. By 1500 the printing press was beginning to work its disturbing and creative effect on European culture. There was a profusion of new universities. Laymen were becoming involved in European intellectual life in increasing numbers and with growing influence, ending a near-monopoly long enjoyed by the clergy. Ideas which may have fizzled out in an earlier age, lost in the introspective atmosphere of a monastic community or confined within the narrow limits of scholastic debate, now stimulated audiences at once larger and more volatile. The ferment was like new wine in the wine cask of medieval traditions, usages, institutions and systems of authority.

Gradually the pressure built up. From about 1300 onwards the political coherence of the medieval world – the unity which it had derived from the catholicity of imperial and papal influences – became progressively more fragile. Most conspicuously, the growth of national political consciousness in France, England and Spain, and the increasing autonomy of sub-national politics in certain Swiss cantons, German princedoms and incorporated cities, eroded papal authority in matters of legal jurisdiction, ecclesiastical taxation, patronage and preferment. And if the secular political ideas of Marsiglio, Machiavelli and others seemed to encourage this trend, religious radicals like Wyclif in England and Hus in Bohemia infuriated their ecclesiastical superiors by seeming to take a perverse delight in it. Indeed, in the fourteenth and fifteenth centuries the institutional integrity of medieval Christendom was threatened as much by the course of ecclesiatical politics as by the secular aspirations of national monarchs. The Avignon exile of the papal court (1309-77), the ensuing schism which dragged on into the

25

fifteenth century, and the subsequent rise of conciliarism within the hierarchy of the Church itself, all illustrated how precarious the medieval Catholic system had become. In retrospect it seems scarcely surprising that after 1517 Luther, Zwingli and Calvin, in company with others, were able to defy the ultimate ecclesiastical sanctions of Rome.

## SECULARIZATION AND THE REFORMATION

The role of the Reformation in the history of secularization was important but ambivalent. Protestantism began as a profoundly religious movement, yet it undoubtedly hastened the transition from medieval Christendom to the more secular environment of Enlightenment Europe. It was in part a rejection of Catholic compromises with Renaissance wordliness and secularity, yet it was at the same time heir to the very spirit of criticism from which the Renaissance had derived its creative energy. Its history illustrates once again the paradox that secularization has no necessary connection with counter-religious ideologies or activities. For without analysing, at this stage, the significance of particular Protestant doctrines and values, it is possible to identify three main areas of European culture in which the Reformation contributed to the secularization processes set in motion at the Renaissance.

First, it left Europeans with a profound crisis of authority. Protestants rejected the magisterium of the Church as the ultimate authority in spiritual and ecclesiastical matters. Whether or not they were right remains a matter of theological argument. Beyond argument, however, is the fact that their iconoclasm weakened permanently the grip which the Christian religion had obtained upon European culture. After the Reformation there was a plurality of contending authority-structures: one still based on the Catholic Church, others derived in various ways from the authority of Scripture, and yet others asserting a variety of mystical and personal revelations. Such fundamental disagreement could hardly fail to promote uncertainty about the authority of religion *per se*. An unresolved crisis of religious authority would lead in the long term to the search for a culture based on purely secular premises. Enlightenment attempts to re-shape consciousness on the basis of human reason, for example, can be seen as radical but inevitable responses to this cultural crisis within which post-Reformation Europe found itself.

Secondly, the Reformation re-imposed upon Europeans a

distinction between Christianity and culture which medieval Christendom had succeeded in obliterating. The ultimate result of this development would be to make religiosity a private, voluntary, individual matter in European societies, and if few sixteenth-century leaders, Protestant or Catholic, either welcomed or even envisaged such a situation, many of their attitudes and innovations certainly anticipated it. The existence of religious diversity introduces an element of choice into religious commitment, and necessarily weakens the automatic, taken-for-granted nature of traditional religious allegiance. Few Reformers conceded freedom of choice to individuals, of course, but German princes, English and French monarchs, and Swiss republicans quickly asserted their right to choose what kind of religiosity would prevail in their communities, and the very existence of alternative modes of Christianity inevitably prompted religious deviance on a scale which persecution could not eradicate. However much the new Protestant sects might wish to impose on their constituents the kind of religious conformity which medieval Catholicism had imposed on earlier generations, circumstances defeated them.

The Reformers made salvation an individual matter. Entry into a Christian community was not by birth but by faith. Affiliation with such a community thus became more personal, more selective, and less automatic. The Calvinistic doctrine of predestination, for example, taught that in a wider society surrounding a community of the elect there would be a population which was not genuinely Christian at all. And while Protestant theology implied that European civilization could no longer be regarded as automatically Christian, Catholic reactions to the Reformation adopted a position which in practice had similar consequences. John Bossy argued in an important article on the emergence of modern Catholicism, published in 1970, that 'a transition from medieval Christianity to modern Catholicism meant, on the popular front, turning collective Christians into individual ones . . . '.[8] For the Tridentine prescriptions which purged and re-invigorated Catholicism did so at the cost of emphasising rites and disciplines which translated traditional community responsibilities into individual types of commitment. The motives were beyond reproach; and the results, wherever this Reformation succeeded, were reflected in the profound devotional quality of Tridentine Catholicism.[9] But where it failed, secular habits often took root in communities now bereft of the traditional assumption – inchoate but nonetheless profound – of a common and ineradicable Christianity.

Finally, the Reformation set in motion various social and political forces leading eventually to religious toleration in most European societies. Both the individualism inherent in the Protestant rejection of Roman authority, and the innate logic of the pluralistic situation itself, dictated a gradual movement (more rapid in some societies than in others) in this direction. The process was very protracted, resolving itself in most cases only in the nineteenth and twentieth centuries. But its secularizing effects began to be felt from the sixteenth century onwards, within both Catholic and Protestant forms of Christianity. The rise of religious toleration – often a *de facto* reality long before it was adopted as official policy of the State – was merely the most obvious manifestation of the decline of religion's once-normative cultural role. Toleration of religious deviance or irreligion implied that religious conformity was regarded no longer as a necessary condition for acceptance within a wider culture. It was an implication which all the major Churches were particularly loath to accept. Certain Anabaptist groups, like later sectarian movements, accepted it readily enough, for they stressed the need for 'gathered churches' to separate themselves from the profane 'world'. But for a State Church toleration was an acknowledgment that the traditional congruence between Christianity and culture had suffered severe erosion.

## PROTESTANTISM, PURITANISM AND SECULARIZATION

The long, erudite debate precipitated by Weber's *The Protestant Ethic and the Spirit of Capitalism*,[10] may not have produced much agreement about the relationship between Protestantism and capitalism, but it certainly has focused attention on that distinctive characteristic of Protestantism which Weber called 'this-worldly asceticism.' As a theological system ascetic Protestantism rested on two basic premises. It stressed the sovereignty of a transcendent God over a rational, ordered creation, and it emphasised individual human responsibilities and prerogatives in matters of faith and practice. Obversely, it pronounced anathema upon magical and superstitious beliefs and rituals which seemed to demean God's sovereignty. Just as the acceptance of monotheism by the ancient Hebrews had unleashed a crusade against graven images, false gods and canaanite rituals, so reformers and puritans, consumed with ideas of divine transcendence and Christian individualism, cast aside much of the cultic paraphernalia of medieval Catholicism. They stripped churches of sacred pictures and relics, and abandoned sacramental practices implying the need for mediation between a believer and his God. It was idolatry, they believed, to invoke and revere the saints of Catholic tradition.

As an historical process, this transition to Protestant asceticism is best understood in terms of Weber's own distinction between the 'virtuoso' religious commitment of the medieval monastic orders and the less intense religiosity of the 'masses'. The ideal monk had been an other-worldly ascetic. While his essential preoccupation had been with the future life, his lifestyle had been rational, methodical and ordered. 'only for him', Weber pointed out, 'did the clock strike, only for him were the hours of the day divided . . . '.[11] Such monastic rationality – unlike the Protestant asceticism of later centuries – was devoted specifically to prayer and meditation in preparation for another world, yet the inescapable fact remained that its ascetic, methodical routines paid mundane dividends for the virtuoso. Indeed, there were no clearer examples of economic rationality in the medieval period than those to be found in monastic communities.

It was therefore most significant that Protestantism rejected the distinction between virtuoso and mass religion. It did away with the dualistic ethics which had made the other-worldly asceticism of the monastery the medieval ideal of the complete Christian. With appeal to a cluster of revolutionary concepts – the idea of the 'priesthood of all believers', the notion of the secular 'calling' and of the 'lay vocation' – Protestantism created a new ethic. Asceticism remained the ideal, but an asceticism of the masses had to function within the 'world'. Sebastian Franck, the German religious radical, was profoundly right when to the early reformers he remarked: 'you think you have escaped from the monastery, but everyone must now be a monk throughout his life'.[12]

Protestantism thus embraced the bold, precarious vision of a world of virtuoso Christians. Entrusting ordinary believers with the responsibilities of priesthood promised either to deepen popular religious devotion or, where that hope failed, to weaken the priestly ideal and office. With the concept of virtuoso religiosity abandoned, in short, the 'Church' faced the alternatives of either sanctifying the 'masses' or being pervaded, more readily than ever before, by the values, norms and beliefs of the wider culture. The only other option would be to isolate itself from the 'world' in a way which medieval Christendom had managed to avoid. This, in the British religious context, was the puritan commitment. Its ideal was to build Christian communities in which all the people would be saints; its mission – as John Wesley put it during his eighteenth-century revival of the puritan legacy – was to 'spread scriptural holiness across the land'.[13] To aim so high, however, was to raise also the price of failure.

Three things made this new, intense brand of Christianity uniquely vulnerable to secularization. The first was its failure to achieve an enduring structure of authority. Protestantism was virtually defenceless, in the long run, against the progressive modification of its original tenets and values by popular cultural forces mediated through the secular involvements of its ordinary members. This chameleon quality could be a strength as well as a weakness, of course; but it did make Protestant religious cultures notably sensitive to secularizing tendencies in their wider societies. Protestantism was not just a religion *for* the masses – that would not have distinguished it from what orthodox Christianity had always been – it was a religion *of* the masses. It would become what its adherents made it, for they were its priests. It had neither Curia nor formal creed; it had no ecclesiastical magisterium to impose authority, no monastic virtuoso to maintain pristine standards of devotion and piety.

Protestantism was open to secularization, secondly, because its nature as a theological system made it an ideal vehicle for philosophical tendencies towards the 'autonomy of man and the world.' If its emphasis on the Christian responsibility and religious competence of the individual believer deprived it of effective corporate authority, its emphasis on divine transcendence initiated a further stage in that rationalization of religious consciousness which Hebrew monotheism had begun and which medieval Catholicism had partially reversed. In the English context the decline of magic provides a useful illustration of this point. It is true that puritan communities often appeared to give credence to magic and witchcraft by the very vigour of their opposition to such things, but closer examination provides evidence of rationalization even in this subterranean area of belief and practice.

To the puritan the Devil remained frightfully real, and one school of puritan theology rationalized the apparent efficacy of witchcraft, folk magic and sorcery by seeing it as diabolical. Another view was that the evil of witches lay in their sacreligious claim to usurp supernatural powers, not in any actual ability to do so. Witches and wizards 'have not power to hurt nor to help us', wrote a puritan authority in 1612, but their practices were detestable nevertheless, for to pretend to supernatural powers was an affront to God's sovereignty over nature. Either way, the impact of puritanism was to emancipate everyday life from a multitude of supernatural assumptions and folk superstitions.[14]

In thus rationalizing the relationship between nature and the supernatural, puritan divines conceived the role of religion in terms considerably more abstract and intangible than it was accorded in the popular consciousness of their society. Folk superstition declined only slowly, particularly in rural communities. But decline it did, and the more rational form of supernaturalism gradually became normative among the kinds of people who embraced ascetic Protestantism in Britain and elsewhere. For such people the age of miracles was considered a thing of the past. The relationship between the human and supernatural worlds was concentrated, in Protestant theology, into one transcendent, historic miracle: the revelation of the Word of God in Christ. All other forms of mediation between the two worlds were rejected. There were no other gods, no unnatural interventions in the modern world, nothing to detract from the awesome majesty of a transcendent deity or to disrupt the natural rhythms of mundane existence.

This is not to say that the English puritan or his European counterpart was less devoutly religious than his Catholic forebears had been. But his was a different kind of religious faith. The *post-mortem* alternatives of eternal bliss or eternal damnation retained a lively influence over his consciousness and behaviour. He detected the hand of God in all the exigencies of life, judging or blessing the motives and achievements of man. But the puritan God worked through the natural order, not by miraculous disruptions of it. If He was accorded new majesty, He was also made more distant in a rational cosmos. Religion remained the dominant expressive force in puritan culture, but for everyday affairs its once-pervasive instrumental significance was trivialized, and its cognitive role became that of an abstract, metaphysical philosophy.

What was the social basis of such ideological changes? A social scientist might argue that the emerging emphasis on divine transcendence was actually a consequence, not just an accompaniment, of that advance of 'secular' knowledge and human mastery over nature which distinguished Western culture in the lead-up to industrialization. Maybe the undeniable intensification of religion as an expressive force was a rationalization and redefinition of religious thought in the face of changing circumstances of human life and knowledge? To this valid suggestion the theologian has an equally valid response. If the world is a wholly 'natural' place, it can still be seen as God's creation; if it is ordered in a rational, empirical way – open to scientific inquiry and manipulated wholly by natural forces, known and unknown – then it is so by divine will, and to those who have eyes to see it declares the glory of its Creator.

At one level this impressive Protestant rationalization of the relationship between 'religious' and 'secular' consciousness was proof against any secularizing tendencies associated with advances in human knowledge and skill – for if God worked through the natural order then all truth was God's truth. Yet at another level, culturally more important, its very philosophical invulnerability as a theological system made Protestantism prey to a more devastating form of secularization. Ideas which defy falsification easily invite indifference. Never, perhaps, had there been a conception of supernatural reality more rational, more sublime, than this one; but neither had there ever been one so utterly dependent on its own intrinsic *a priori* plausibility. Making no cognitive or instrumental claims to assist its adherents in the day-to-day experiences of the natural world, Protestantism – if ever it lost its historic appeal as an expressive force, and its evident utility as a source of social and institutional cohesion – would face the kind of crisis of plausibility which has become familiar to twentieth-century Christianity. Its relevance, not its truth, would be at stake.

Ironically, then, the third aspect of the Protestant religion which intrudes into a history of secularization is its complex involvement in the 'modernization' of western culture. As various historians have pointed out, there was no necessary connection between the theology of the sixteenth-century reformers and the kinds of habits and assumptions which produced 'worldly asceticism',[15] but there can be little doubt that the twin emphasis on divine sovereignty and human responsibility in Calvinism and puritanism did serve to legitimate the ascetic virtues of work, thrift and productive investment – at least for the kinds of people who were attracted to such movements. To 'legitimate' something is not to create it, but to make it more readily acceptable in a society which might otherwise react with suspicion or hostility. This was the crux of the association between Protestantism and capitalism. Capitalism was neither created by Protestantism nor necessarily dependent on it for success, but Protestantism was, in many instances, an important factor in the adjustment of individuals and social groups to the norms and values of the capitalist system.

For from the Protestant tendency to view lay occupations in vocational terms – as a 'calling' – it was an obvious step to emphasise work as an aspect of Christian stewardship and to see material success as a token of divine favour. There was nothing novel about appreciating the moral value of work, but ascetic Protestants saw profit, and work as a source of profit, in a new light. To English puritans, and later to the followers of John Wesley, not only was idleness a sin, but temporal improvement was also a godly ambition. 'Gain all you can', Wesley reiterated in sermon after sermon. Plainly, if less often, he echoed the injunction of Richard Baxter's *Christian Directory*, which had warned its puritan readers:

If God show you a way in which you may lawfully get more than in another way (without wrong to your soul or to any other), if you refuse this, and choose the less gainful way, you cross one of the ends of your Calling, and you refuse to be God's steward.[16]

That such exhortations were accompanied so often by dire warnings against hedonism and the love of wealth for its own sake is noteworthy, not only to give a balanced picture of Protestant values, but also as an index of the success of the movement as a catalyst of economic growth. Wesley was sure, from observation, that 'wherever true Christianity spreads, it must cause diligence and frugality, which, in the natural course of things, must beget riches'![17] He feared, with good reason, for the spiritual fidelity of materialistic, acquisitive Christians, without ever finding a satisfactory prescription for halting the growth of these things in an ascetic religious culture. Indeed, in the history of secularization a salient aspect of Protestantism has been the virtual impossibility, in communities dominated by laity, of effectively combining positive attitudes to worldly success with negative attitudes to 'worldliness'. A broad road has led from 'this-worldly asceticism' into a mundane, bourgeois complacency which is neither ascetic nor religious.

## THE ENLIGHTENMENT AND THE RISE OF SECULAR HUMANISM

The 'Weber thesis' has prompted vigorous arguments about the philosophical sympathies of Benjamin Franklin, the great eighteenth-century American whom Weber cited as an exemplar of that 'spirit of capitalism' which he linked with Protestant asceticism. Was Franklin an ascetic Protestant or a man of the Enlightenment? Opinions differ, and Franklin's *Autobiography* is open to divergent interpretations. The specific example need not delay the present analysis, but the very fact that the issue is so blurred is most illuminating. For the difference between the 'this-worldly rationality' of Protestantism and the secular rationality of the Enlightenment could devolve in practice into little more than a question of metaphysical orientation. Both stressed the efficacy of human endeavours to master the physical world and improve it. Both distinguished firmly between secular and religious modes of thought, albeit for very different reasons. And among the reasons for the flowering of scientific thought in post-Reformation Europe was the cross-fertilization of ascetic Protestantism both with

33

the older humanistic values of the Renaissance and with the bouyant intellectual optimism of the 'Age of Reason'.

But if in the practical processes of 'modernization' – and therefore secularization – developments in European religion anticipated and later reinforced the effects of secular ideologies based on reason, there the complementarity ended. The Enlightenment was a rejection of the kind of compromise between secular and religious thought which Protestantism offered. It took to a logical conclusion the process of philosophical rationalization which the Renaissance had begun, and by so doing forced Protestantism into the same kind of defensive posture which the Reformation had imposed on the Catholic Church. For if the Reformation had destroyed the unitary religious culture of Christendom, the Enlightenment broke the basic Christian consensus which the Reformation crisis had left fragile but intact. Secularization had entered a new phase.

To speak of a Christian consensus in pre-Enlightenment Europe is to emphasise the absence of acceptable alternatives to beliefs and values traditionally associated with Christianity. To be a non-Christian was to be an ideological deviant. Protestantism had become in many areas a legitimate alternative to Catholicism, but to Christianity itself there was no alternative. It remained normative everywhere. The Europe of 1600 or 1650 was not, of course, peopled entirely by devout and literal Christian believers – a cursory reading of Shakespeare, for example, gives the lie to such a notion, particularly if it chances on his treatment of immortality. Yet the Christian worldview did remain the prevailing orthodoxy, to be taken as seriously as inclination or circumstances dictated. It was still, among educated and uneducated alike, the 'taken-for-granted' way of understanding reality; of finding a larger meaning in life. There did not yet exist the kind of philosophical framework around which a secular culture might develop.

It was in providing such a framework that the Enlightenment became one of the great discontinuities in European history. Like all historical events, it was a culmination as well as a beginning. The secularizing tendencies of the Renaissance and the Reformation had made it possible, both intellectually and politically. Intellectually, for example, as the Reformation debates had hardened into Catholic and Protestant orthodoxies, the unresolved crisis of religious authority had nurtured newer, more radical kinds of criticism and inquiry. The scientific work of Copernicus, Galileo and Kepler, and the frankly heretical speculations of men like Nicholas of Cusa and Giordano Bruno, had prompted growing doubts about the plausibliity of the traditional Christian cosmology; and during the second half of the seventeenth century other scholars, less well remembered than the great pioneers of science, had established nagging literary and historical doubts about the chronological accuracy (and therefore literal veracity) of the Old Testament. And at the same time, expanding European contacts with non–Christian cultures, notably in China, and a growing scholarly awareness of overlaps between Judaism and the 'heathen' religions of Near Eastern antiquity, had begun to raise even more fundamental questions about the now-precarious Christian consensus.[18]

Politically, the background to the Enlightenment was the aftermath of debilitating 'Wars of Religion', in which the legal and moral authority of religious institutions and religious functionaries had sunk to a very low ebb. From the English Civil War to the Revolution of 1688 religion had been a key factor in British politics, but the period had ended with an almost total elimination of Anglicanism's once-formidable power as an independent social and political institution. On the Continent, over a century of conflict had ended in 1648 with a similar prostration of the Catholic, Lutheran and Reformed Churches. In much of Europe, then, statesmen were under little pressure to uphold the traditional Christian consensus by political means. Indeed, the ready exchange of the seventeenth-century Absolutist appeal to 'Divine Right' theory for the secular ideologies preferred by eighteenth-century Enlightened despots suggests positive political encouragement of the new thought. The radical doubts and anti-Christian speculations of men like Voltaire, Pierre Bayle, John Toland or David Hume could, for the first time since the Christianization of Europe, be disseminated and embraced without fear of political persecution or general social opprobrium.

But the Enlightenment was only a beginning. In the period after about 1680 opponents and protagonists of new, distinctly secular ways of interpreting the material world and understanding human nature began, in Paul Hazard's words, 'fighting desperately for the possession of men's souls, confronting each other in a contest at which the whole of thoughtful Europe was looking on.'[19] The authority of Christianity was not just being ignored – that would have created no precedent – it was being contradicted. The assailants may have remained a small, sophisticated minority, but their influence on Europe's educated elite was enormous, and even their foremost opponents found little heart to dispute their proprietorial attitude to the future. In their exuberance, however, the prophets of Enlightenment underestimated the magnitude of their task. In the short term, at least, they lost the battle for the European mind. It is instructive to compare the mood of Bishop

Butler's *Analogy of Religion*, a masterly defence of the Christian position published in 1736 at the height of the Enlightenment debate in England, with Edmund Burke's evaluation half a century later. Butler took the pessimistic view that the battle was being lost, for in his opinion 'among all people of discernment' religious belief was held to be 'fictious'.[20] Burke's picture of the English culture of the 1790s was one in which 'atheists and infidels' had slipped into 'lasting oblivion'. 'Who, born within the last forty years,' he asked rhetorically,

has read one word of Collins, and Toland, and Tindal, and Chubb, and Morgan, and that whole race who called themselves Freethinkers? Who now reads Bolingbroke? Who ever read him through? Ask the booksellers of London what is become of all these lights of the world. In as few years their few successors will go to the family vault of 'all the Capulets'.[21]

Neither Butler nor Burke spoke with complete authenticity for the spirit of his age, but the contrast does capture the historical process through which the Enlightenment battle for 'men's souls' changed from a heady assault into a subtle war of attrition. Demolishing the basis of a civilization and replacing it with something new is not the work of a single generation or a few decades. To maintain a proper historical perspective of secularization we must remember that today, in the final quarter of the twentieth century, and with the Enlightenment 300 years in the past, neither the dechristianization of Europe nor the construction of an autonomous secular culture is either complete or certain. Christian beliefs and values not only survived the Enlightenment, but retained a dominant (if somewhat token) influence within the establishment cultures of most European countries long after the specific controversies raised by Enlightenment thought had been overtaken by fresh issues and new problems.

While it remained *dominant*, however, the Christian worldview was no longer *normative*. This was the crucial change produced by the intellectual ferment of the late-seventeenth and early-eighteenth centuries. The Christian consensus, although strained by doubt, ignorance and complacency, had held sway up to the Enlightenment: the post-Enlightenment West was a pluralistic culture. The importance of the Enlightenment thus lay in its negative, iconoclastic impact on contemporary consciousness. The philosophical systems of the 'Age of Reason' produced no satisfactory substitute for the Christian consensus which they had undermined, but although the intense counter-religious animus of early rationalism tended to disappear, there could be no return to the old unitary culture. The evolution of Western consciousness had entered a new, modern phase.

With few exceptions, at a philosophical level 'modernity' has meant doubt, uncertainty and dissensus. Not only did Enlightenment rationalism fail as a substitute for traditionally integrative religious assumptions, it also generated a host of secular philosophies to compete with each other, as well as with Europe's continuing religious traditions, for control of modern consciousness. Faith in human reason has, of course, persisted as part of the 'taken-for-granted' intellectual heritage of modern culture, with its currency underwritten by the scientific and technological ethos of modern industrial civilisation; but to the 'wasteland' mentality of much modern thought the 'Age of Reason' seems a naive and falsely optimistic epoch, and neither idealism nor positivism has ever succeeded in imposing new rationalistic norms on Western culture as a whole.[22]

The persistence, even in decline, of Christian supernaturalism has been a factor in this failure, as has the emergence or intrusion of various forms of mysticism and non-Christian spirituality. But secular critiques of rationalism have operated even more powerfully against it. The initial eighteenth-century protest of romantic naturalism has often been re-echoed, especially in anarchistic or arcadian forms of counter-cultural reaction to industrialization. For while Romanticism has always embraced a wide range of philosophical positions and asthetic orientations, its underlying affirmation of what Nietzsche called 'the wisdom of the body' – its insistence on the creative vitality of the human will and the transcendence of non-rational forms of reality – has appeared repeatedly to exploit the evident failure of rationalism to explain the complexities and contradictions of individual and social behaviour in the modern world. Marxism, too, has challenged aspects of the traditionl rationalist outlook, for its emphasis on the role of economic forces which human reason may rationalize but cannot create or ultimately control questions aspects of both idealistic and naturalistic forms of rationalism. And in the present century the sub-rational hedonism of Freudian psychology and (in a different way), the implications of existentialism, have added to that epistemological confusion which is modern western culture's alternative to the Christian consensus of an earlier age.

But while it may be epistemologically confused, 'modernity' is at the same time emphatically secular, and for all its diversity the post-Enlightenment cultural tradition has been almost uniformly secularizing in its impact on European consciousness. Exceptions such as the much-observed European fascination with Eastern religions, or the residual influence of superstition and the sporadic appearance of new forms of mystical and transcendental spirituality have been but relatively minor currents in a broadening stream which now seems to dwarf the older Christian tradition. From a Christian viewpoint the whole process can appear more like a concerted movement of secularization than a fragmentary development of contending ideological systems. And in a real sense it has been so. Certain basic 'modern' dispositions – the rejection of religious authority, the abandonment of attitudes of mind ascribing instrumental or cognitive significance to the supernatural, and the re-fashioning of European consciousness in terms of the autonomy of man and the primacy of this-worldly existence – these things have in fact transcended most of the ideological divisions in modern Western thought.

Secular humanism, in one form or another, has become the dominant modern worldview. Alexander Pope's famous couplet,

Know then thyself, presume not God to scan;

The proper study of mankind is Man,[23]

expressed perfectly the amalgam of humanism and secular consciousness which was to become the lasting legacy of the Enlightenment. Its values and assumptions, which pervaded both Rationalism and Romanticism and gave a certain unity to the diversity of subsequent philosophical developments, have also become more or less normative in the arts and social sciences. And it is ironic that possibly the clearest evidence of the nearly irresistible force of secular humanism is to be found within the very religious tradition whose normative role it has usurped. For in the quest for relevance in the modern world, Christian theologians have been drawn in increasing numbers to the logic of Feuerbach's dictum that, to remain valid, all theology must be transformed into anthropology.[24]

Such an example is useful partly because it illustrates that secular humanism need not be anti-religious in any conscious sense. The aggressive, 'secularist' animus of the Enlightenment has given way, in a more pluralistic culture, to philosophical assumptions which weakened religious consciousness not by attacking 'religious' modes of thought, but by ignoring them. The traditional imperative to define ultimate reality in supernatural, other-worldly terms, and to ground human systems of knowledge and authority in transcendental principles of one kind or another, has relaxed gradually. Modern preoccupations are less metaphysical, less univeral, less abstract. They are focussed more narrowly on aspects of empirical reality, natural law, and the pursuit of temporal happiness – all of which imply tacit assumptions about the practical autonomy of man and the world. Thus the typical evidence of secularization in a culture based on secular humanism is not a growth of atheism, or even agnosticism, but a general tendency for people ideologically uncommitted on religious issues to become almost entirely alienated from the modes of thought and definitions of reality which have made religiosity explicable and relevant in the past.

Surveying the history of ideas is like drawing a roadmap and leaving out the details of topography, demography and economic development which make sense of the pattern abstracted in the map. The survey, like the roadmap, nevertheless provides valuable clues to the interplay of material and human factors underlying the abstraction. This chapter has tried to map the major trends in Western attitudes to religion since the Renaissance, and by so doing to draw attention to the basic problems of explanation raised by the familiar pattern of rationalization and disenchantment. What made particular generations critical of ideas and values which had long been taken for granted? What kinds of changes enabled radical notions about nature and supernature to win widespread acceptance in societies which earlier rejected them as nonsense or heresy? How are we to account for the evident relationship between the modernization of Western societies and the secular trend towards 'the autonomy of man and the world'?

In the search for answers the analysis now turns to the central phenomenon in the modernization process – the Industrial Revolution – and to the British context in which industrialization began. The crucial task will be to explore links between the secularization of culture and the profound transformation which has occurred in the material circumstances and social structures of British life. For even on the doubtful assumption that an intellectual minority might be moved by the force of abstract philosophical arguments alone, the problem remains of explaining the popularization of the new, secular consciousness amongst the masses of ordinary citizens whose worldview is much more likely to be shaped by change or continuity in the interests, prejudices, values and satisfactions arising from the concrete realities and experiences of everyday life.

## NOTES

1. Thomas, K. (1973), p. 51.
2. The best source may still be Burckhardt, J. (1944), but cf. also Koyrs, A. (1968), Mandrou, R. (1978) and de Santillana, G. (1956).
3. Quoted by de Santillana (1956), p. 12.
4. Quoted by Singer, C. (1959), p. 169.
5. Quoted by Rattansi, P. M. (1972), p. 16.

6. Ibid.
7. Ullmann, W. (1965), p. 208.
8. Bossy, J. (1970), p. 62.
9. As illustrated, e.g., in Bossy's own work, Ibid., *passim*, and Bossy, J. (1977), pp. 129-37. See also Evennett, H. O. (1968), pp. 23-42, 67-88.
10. Green, R.W. (1959) still provides a good summary of the debate; but see also Samuelsson, K. (1961); Trevor-Roper, H. (1967); and, of course, Weber, M. (1930).
11. Weber, M. (1930), p. 178, pp. 155-83.
12. Ibid., p. 179.
13. *Minutes of the Methodist Conferences from the First, Held in London, by the late Rev. John Wesley, A.M., in the Year 1744*, vol. 1, London, 1862, p. 449.
14. Thomas, K. (1973), pp. 58-89, 681-98.
15. For example, Robertson, H. M. (1933), Sombart, W. (1915) and Tawney, R. H. (1938), especially pp. 311-13.
16. *Christian Directory*, 1678, vol. 1, p. 378b. Quoted by Tawney, R. H. (1938).
17. Wesley, John (1876), vol. 3, p. 325.
18. Hazard, P. (1973), pp. 27-72.
19. Ibid., p. 9.
20. Quoted by Wood, A. S. (1960), p. 15.
21. Burke, Edmund (1909), p. 225.
22. For the purposes of a discussion of religious consciousness perhaps the most profound exploration of these themes is in Neibuhr, Reinhold (1941), vol. I, pp. 1-131. Cf. Dawson, C. (1945), *passim*.
23. *Essay of Man*, II. The poem was written in 1733.
24. Feuerbach, L. (1854), pp. xxxvii-xxxix.

# PART TWO

# The post-Christian world

'The movement beginning about the thirteenth century (I am not going to get involved in any arguments about the exact date) towards the autonomy of man (under which head I place the discovery of the laws by which the world lives and manages in science, social and political affairs, art, ethics and religion) has in our time reached a certain completion. Man has learned to cope with all questions of importance without recourse to God as a working hypothesis.'

(Dietrich Bonhoeffer, *Letters and Papers from Prison*)

# The great discontinuity

The Britain whose intellectuals wrestled with the challenge of Enlightenment thought in the early eighteenth century was a society on the brink of rapid transformation and expansion. What might have been the fate of Enlightenment attitudes and philosophies in the absence of these accompanying events remains conjectural, but clearly, once successful industrialization had begun it dominated social and cultural developments in Britain. Without it there would have been little opportunity for significant penetration by secular humanism beyond the perimeters of that wealthy, leisured intelligentsia fascinated already by the novelty of secular ideas and assumptions. In the emergent industrial society, however, such penetration went hand in hand with other aspects of a profound societal transformation. For once the 'take-off' point had been passed – once industrialization had become a self-sustaining economic 'revolution' – an accompanying 'modernization' was bound to influence the evolution of British life at all levels, and often to dictate it.

## INDUSTRIALIZATION AND MODERNIZATION

Industrial revolution produced a great discontinuity in human history, and led to the emergence of distinctively 'modern' types of culture and social structure. No other events, neither major international conflicts nor spectacular political revolutions, have exercised a comparable influence on human life and human thought. In Britain, the first industrial nation, the discontinuity was in many ways less abrupt, less conspicuous, than it would be in countries like Germany, Russia or

Japan, where subsequent processes of industrialization had the patterns and achievements of successful industrialization to compete with and emulate. Yet British society was transformed as a result of the classical 'Industrial Revolution' which dominated the half-century after about 1780. Scholars will no doubt continue to argue about the amount of historical continuity between the methods, economic enterprises and social attitudes of pre-industrial times and those of the Industrial Revolution; and certainly it is possible to argue that neither the systematic use of technology to harness non-animal sources of energy nor the medium of factory production was entirely novel during the closing decades of the eighteenth century. Yet it remains appropriate to call this a 'revolution'. For industrial production, with all its profound implications for consciousness and behaviour, began for the first time in history to dominate a whole society – to dictate its way of life.

An Industrial Revolution creates economic growth on a scale unprecedented. It encourages and requires radical changes in the social structures, settlement patterns and living standards of a society. And as a cultural force its effect is to 'modernize' attitudes, values, expectations and social relationships, and to subvert traditional assumptions not readily adaptable to the circumstances of an industrial age. Here, in human terms, lies the greatest discontinuity of all. For not just as an economic and material transformation, but equally as a social and cultural phenomenon, successful industrialization can appropriately be regarded as a watershed in human experience with which only the Neolithic Revolution of prehistory is comparable.[1] For an historian interested in the emergence of a modern, increasingly secular 'world', it is to this great discontinuity that the analysis inevitably is drawn.

Such an historian cannot avoid the idea of 'modernization', even if he eschews the actual word. Used here as a summary description for a complex, integrated and linear process of societal change, the term itself does require certain elaboration. For while 'modernization' is an expressive word, it is also a contentious one. Throughout the 1950s and 1960s the development of modernization theory was dominatied by scholars concerned chiefly with the practical application of economic models to Third World countries approaching industrialization. Controversy resulted, for in such contexts the word lost the neutral tone which it had acquired in the work of the classical sociologists. Too often it seemed to imply the innate superiority of Western values and institutions, or to go hand in hand with a bland, uncritical acceptance of industrialization.

'Modernization' is used in this study on the assumption that it remains useful simply as a description of an actual historical process.

But the controversy which its use has aroused can serve to teach important lessons about the nature of secularization. For scholars who regard secularization as a linear and irreversible historical trend are guilty of the same kind of assumption as that made by proponents of modernization theory who present industrialization and modernization as beneficient and irreversible developments. The point is that, historically, neither assumption is legitimate. For while on the one hand history is not a predictive science, on the other there are obvious features of the modern (and secular) societies of the West which suggest the impermanence, not the irreversibility, of recent societal developments.

The historic confluence of industrialization and modernization may indeed prove to be a transient, disastrous, even terminal phase in human history. If the Promethean fire fuelled by awesome energy sources and advanced technologies does not eventually destroy the world which it has created, it may in time be extinguished by it own voracious depletion of the earth's resources. Either way, the whole basis of 'modern' society would collapse. There is therefore something ironic in the sanguinity with which Harold Perkin, in *The Origins of Modern English Society*, explained that industrialization is an irreversible process. An Industrial Revolution, he wrote, is

a unique phase of historical development: the one-way road which, if travelled successfully, leads from the undeveloped society's comparative poverty, insecurity, and dependence on the bounty of nature to the comparative wealth, security and freedom of choice of the developed society.

Why a 'one-way road'? Because, Perkin argued, 'any return to lower levels of productiveness would involve a catastrophe of such magnitude as almost certainly to bring down civilization with it, if not to destroy human life itself. . . '[2] But this is a curious argument. Something is not irreversible simply because reversal would involve catastrophe. Indeed, in the decade since *The Origins of Modern English Society* appeared many 'experts' have in fact concluded that the economic and social trends set in train by industrialization will terminate with the doomsday of modern civilization.

The notion that secularization is irreversible[3] is similarly precarious. As a process advanced by the confluence of industrialization and modernization, it may yet be, with them, speedily reversed, although at a price likely to dampen the enthusiasm of all but the most *religiose* of observers. On the other hand, until such a reversal occurs, 'modernization' seems destined to remain the underlying tendency of social and cultural development in industrialized societies such as Britain, and its nature must be understood if we are to understand the post-Christian world. 'Modern' tendencies did not originate with the Industrial Revolution, of course. (Chapter Two of this study has been concerned to examine pre-industrial trends which led Western civilization towards modern, secular beliefs and values.) But with the 'great discontinuity' of Industrial Revolution, 'modernization' became a powerful, pervasive influence capable, in time, of transforming the whole structure of society.

Among the most important features of 'modernity' it is possible to identify the following basic developments:

- Unprecedented economic productivity associated with the systematic, largescale exploitation of non-animal sources of energy;
- A massive sustained growth of knowledge and technical skill, combined with the progressive application of new technology;
- A related sophistication in the methods and content of education, coupled with reduced familial involvement in education and production;
- Urbanization, including the growth of varieties of semi-urban settlement;
- The growth of competing, pluralistic systems of social stratification, together with the progressive differentiation of roles, skills and decision-making institutions;
- A combination of increased personal mobility, both spatial and social, with vastly improved systems of communication and transport, including mass media of various types;
- Bureaucratization, including both a vast increase in the scale and complexity of government, and the emergence of largescale administrative bureaucracies performing non-governmental functions in such areas as commerce, insurance, welfare and recreation; and
- A rationalization of the relationship between work and leisure, so that the two are differentiated clearly in time, in location, and (often) in a related separation of the social networks involved.

The list might be extended, or arranged in different ways, but the basic characteristics distinguishing a modern industrial society from earlier, or alternative, social systems, are subsumed under these categories.

Yet it is a summary confined to the social dimension of modernization, and as such remains skeletal. The human experience of modernization – the beliefs and values, hopes and fears, symbols and myths which have evolved to give human meaning and substance to the modern world – the making, in short, of a modern culture – has involved a departure from the pre-industrial past even more fundamental than the social discontinuities which are so prominent. Secularization has operated at both levels. Chapter Four, which follows, will concentrate on the cultural aspect, seeking to explain why 'secular' consciousness and modern culture apparently go hand in hand. Chapter Five will then proceed to examine relationships between social changes and secularization in modern Britain.

## NOTES

1. Various historians have made this comparison, including, for example, Cipolla, C. (1962), pp. 17-31, and Perkin, H. (1969), pp. 4-5.
2. Perkin, H. (1969), p. 4.
3. The well-known American sociologist of religion, Peter Berger, is an exponent of this view, arguing that the assumption that secularization will not be reversed is among the 'safest' of sociological predictions. See, for example, Berger, P. (1967), pp. 3ff.

# CHAPTER THREE

# The emergence of a secular culture

At the beginning of the Victorian era, as the early industrial period drew to a close in Britain, the great material changes and social developments of the previous half-century were beginning to spawn a new and largely secular culture. In a useful article on what he has called 'The Ethical Revolt against Christian Orthodoxy in Early Victorian England', Howard R. Murphy has sought to identify one aspect of this development by making use of George Bernard Shaw's distinction between 'meliorism' and 'salvationism'. Where previously most human beings had taken for granted a view of the world as a 'vale of tears' to be negotiated 'on the way to eternal bliss or eternal damnation', there was beginning to emerge among the early Victorians, Murphy suggests, 'the idea that the world was susceptible to systematic improvement through a sustained application of human effort and intelligence.'[1]

Like most historical arguments based on contrast concepts, this analysis over-simplifies the realities of cultural change, but it succeeds nevertheless in drawing attention to a crucial ingredient of the emerging 'modern' culture. Melioristic attitudes to life were not new. Enlightenment thought, for example, had thrived on them. But never before had they made obvious commonsense to large sections of a society. The Industrial Revolution, in short, was in the process of making meliorism popular, and in calling this the 'Age of Improvement' Asa Briggs has shrewdly echoed the dominant theme in early industrial consciousness.[2] It was a novel theme for ordinary Britons. In the past, under economic systems of slow growth or no-growth, an accumulation of material wealth and comfort by some members of a society had been possible only at the expense of the many. Worldly rewards and satisfactions, for most human beings, had been circumscribed by the more or less static nature of the material culture, and plagued by what Perkin has called 'the tyranny and niggardliness of nature'.[3] Then, rather suddenly, the self-sustaining economic growth of an industrial economy had 'opened the road for men to complete mastery of their physical environment, without the inescapable need to exploit each other'.[4]

Human values and attitudes to the world were bound to change in response to this development. Perkin, who more than most recent historians has stressed the integral relationship between material, social and cultural aspects of the phenomenon, has no doubt about the linkage between the material abundance of an industrial economy and the distinctive character of modern culture. 'If life and the ends of life are more than the material means', he has concluded, then industrialization must be seen as a 'more than material revolution', for 'in principle, at least, it made it possible that all men might have life, and might have it more abundantly, in that wider choice of ends hitherto restricted to the few'.[5] In practice, of course, industrialization produced victims as well as beneficiaries. It brought new forms of exploitation in its train. Throughout the nineteenth century, and indeed up to the present day, sections of British industrial society – the old, the unemployed, the unskilled or semi-skilled, the individuals or occupational groups unprotected by property or unionization – have continued to face misery and hardship born of poverty and economic insecurity. Yet the fact of dramatic 'improvement' cannot be gainsaid, nor can the evidence that it has been sufficiently pervasive to have effected a general transformation of values and expectations.

This vital development in the secularization of British culture is perhaps best elaborated by considering the three classical 'breaking-points' at which human efforts to control the world, and win autonomy from nature, have always met defeat. The key words are *powerlessness, poverty* and *contingency*. There can be no more effective counter to the melioristic assumption that the world can be improved through human effort, or to the growth of the kind of 'secular' consciousness which typically accompanies meliorism, than an environment confronting its human inhabitants with blunt, inescapable reminders of their vulnerability and weakness in an unpredictable universe. As Chapter One has argued, where such 'breaking-points' make more or less constant intrusion into human affairs, the prevailing culture is likely to be highly susceptible to 'religious' modes of thought.

# 'SALVATIONISM' AND SOCIETY

In pre-industrial Britain a popular pamphlet entitled, significantly, *An Appeal to Common Sense in Behalf of Religion*, could count on a good deal of resonance between its metaphysical assumptions and the prevailing worldview. Other-worldliness made common sense. 'The great truths of religion are so consonant to the natural sentiments of the human mind, and the opposite absurdities are so ridiculous', wrote the Rev James Oswald in 1768, 'that one would think it impossible for any man of sense to hesitate in admitting the one, and rejecting the other. . . .' Why? Because, wrote Oswald, no more indubitable truths could be presented to the human mind than the truth 'That life is uncertain, and that death is certain.' Yet religion suffered, he admitted, because only when reminders of these facts remained obvious and ubiquitous would people overcome a 'natural' tendency to neglect religion in favour of mundane, worldly preoccupations. 'When alarming symptoms appear,' the argument concluded, 'we are then strong believers, because we are apt to believe the evils we fear; but when the fight is over, we entertain the contrary opinion on the slightest grounds imaginable. . . .'[6] There could be no clearer theoretical framework than this in which to analyse the religious-cultural consequences of modernization.

For although well-off by pre-industrial standards, the Britain inherited by Oswald's generation never was really free from 'alarming symptoms' of human finitude frailty and insecurity. Keith Thomas's brilliant analysis of the physical and social environment of pre-industrial culture presents a picture as clear as it is sombre. We see a population which was, by modern standards, 'exceedingly liable to pain, sickness and premature death'.[7] Even among the aristocracy, one infant in three failed to live to the age of five, and life expectancy at birth around the time of the Restoration was not quite thirty years.[8] It was a society dependent on a precarious food supply, on the recurrent contingency of an annual harvest which appears to have been a total failure as frequently as one year in six, and which even at the best of times left a majority of the people with debilitating vitamin deficiencies.[9] These factors, combined with a notable 'lack of hygiene, ignorance of antiseptics and absence of effective sanitation', meant that diseases like rickets, anaemia, tuberculosis and gastric infection were virtually endemic, and that the society was terribly vulnerable to periodic epidemics of influenza, typhus, dysentry and smallpox.[10]

Pre-industrial existence was a 'vale of tears' not simply because dirt, disease and death were so prominent, but because its frequent crises were at once inexplicable and uncontrollable – at least in human, mundane terms. Medicine was not only without effective *cures* (a person entering a hospital as a patient 'would certainly be increasing his chances of contracting some fatal infection')[11]; it was also without satisfactory *explanations*. Until the cholera epidemics of the nineteenth century the terrible onslaught of epidemic disease could be explained only as a visitation of divine wrath, and in face of the daily struggle against lesser ailments pre-industrial communities continued to find comfort, if not success, by resort to magical remedies and supernatural explanations. Outside the ranks of a small intelligentsia, in short this world remained an 'enchanted garden': capricious, dangerous, mysterious. And quite apart from the constant threat of death and disease, it was a world full of dangers and uncertainties against which a more sophisticated, wealthier industrial society would be able to fashion institutional safeguards and insurances. Fire, for example, was a dire threat to life and livelihood, yet it was a disaster so common – so difficult to avert with the kinds of heating and lighting which the society required – that at the outbreak of the great fire in London in 1666 only those in its immediate vicinity took much notice.[12]

## THE SOCIAL ORIGINS OF MELIORISM

This daunting pre-industrial environment was not, of course, either static or constant. At every social level the British were, by most standards, better-off than their social equivalents across the English Channel or the Irish Sea; and their own experience of life fluctuated both with long-term patterns of climate, demography and epidemic virulence, and with short-term cycles of bounty and scarcity at harvest. Moreover, some 'improvement' was in evidence in the century before the Industrial Revolution, most of it in association with social and economic trends which, in turn, were part of a general movement towards industrial 'take off'. Nevertheless, the comprehensive, holistic transformation leading to the distinctive environment of modern life was fundamentally dependent on effective industrialization, and for that reason has been confined to the period since the mid-nineteenth century. Its most important characteristics must be examined as part of the background to the growth of melioristic, secular values and expectations in the modern world.

## Standards of living

With industrialization was associated, over the long term, an enormous increase in the standard of living of almost all members of British society. Prolonged and heated debate has raged over the standard of living of the labouring classes during the period from the 1790s to the 1840s, but even if we conclude – with the so-called 'pessimists' – first, that the lot of many sections of these classes deteriorated during the early industrial age, secondly, that if there was an overall improvement it was at best marginal, and finally, that in any case there were formidable social costs to be paid for material improvement, two things remain beyond dispute. On the one hand, it is certain that *after* the 1840s even the labouring classes were sharing, not fully but certainly significantly, in the material rewards of the Industrial Revolution. And on the other, during the entire period of industrialization the society as a whole became rapidly more wealthy: primary production, national industrial production, domestic consumption, per capita income, and national earnings from international trade and finance all far outstripped population growth.[13]

Economic expectations changed accordingly. 'Every man is rich or poor', Adam Smith had explained in 1776, 'according to the degree in which he can afford to enjoy the necessaries, conveniences, and amusements of human life'.[14] On this criterion, by the middle of the nineteenth century the ranks of the very wealthy had been swelled, the numbers and wealth of the British middle classes had grown so rapidly that the whole society seemed bound to take on a bourgeois character, and it had become possible for ambitious members of the working classes to emulate middle-class patterns of consumption and to share middle-class expectations of continuing economic improvement.[15] During the next half-century, while average real wages rose by 84 per cent and average retail prices fell by 11 per cent, the range of 'conveniences' and 'amusements' in the domestic market widened steadily. Nor did the process halt or decelerate in the twentieth century. Indeed, despite the economic uncertainties of the 1960s and 1970s, the availability of material wealth and comforts in contemporary Britain separates the citizens of today from the material culture of their grandparents far more decisively than their grandparents' world had advanced beyond that of the eighteenth century.

The functions of the automobile and the aeroplane, electric lighting and the vast accumulation of labour-saving devices powered by electricity, the impact of the telephone, radio, television receiver and telecommunications satellite, the taken-for-granted role of the computer, the laser and the nuclear reactor, and the widespread application of chemical and biochemical discoveries in the fields of plastics, textiles, architecture and medicine, are among the most obvious of the pervasive technological changes which have made the modern world, in industrial societies, a material environment unique in the history of the human species. Even the least wealthy members of contemporary British society, with relatively few exceptions, have access to a quality and quantity of material comforts, consumer items and services which not even the wealthy could have imagined just a century ago.

## Health and longevity

Rising living standards were parallelled by improvements in nutrition, in the prevention and treatment of diseases, and in the quality of infant and child care. Human knowledge and skill were not always decisive factors in these improvements. The modern decline in mortality rates, for example, appears to have begun around the middle of the eighteenth century as a result of a fortuitous combination of agricultural prosperity, improved facilities for the supply of foodstuffs when local shortages did occur, and (between the smallpox epidemics of the late 1720s and the coming of cholera in 1832), a surprisingly long period of exemption from serious epidemic disease. But after about 1850 Britain was in the forefront of a medical revolution in which all nations eventually shared.

Medicine became a science. James Simpson of Edinburgh successfully anaesthetized a patient with chloroform in 1847. Twenty years later Joseph Lister introduced new antiseptic methods for eliminating infection during surgery. Louis Pasteur, meanwhile, had laid the basis for anti-bacterial medicine with discoveries to which British doctors were quickly attracted. In 1896 the clinical use of X-rays began. In the second decade of the twentieth century the grim realities of war prompted further advances in surgical medicine, in the understanding of infection, and in the science of sanitation. More recently, dramatic achievements have accompanied the discovery of penicillin, the subsequent development of a potent range of antibiotic and chemotherapeutic drugs, the perfecting of micro-surgical techniques, and the beginnings of effective organ transplants.

Medicine also became more thoroughly professional. During the past century doctors, nurses, hospital administrators and other paramedical personnel have become subject to rigorous standards of training and procedure. There has been a marked improvement in the sanitation of cities, schools and public buildings, accompanied by growing public knowledge about the rudiments of personal and family health. Despite chronic problems and sporadic crises, the same period has seen an increased availability of medical services to the society as a whole. However history finally evaluates the National Health scheme of the past thirty years, there can be no doubt about the overall improvement of public health during the industrial age. Compared with the life expectancy of 29.6 years of an infant born into the aristocracy – the most favoured class – about 300 years ago, in Britain in 1975 the life expectancy at birth of the average male was 69.3 years, and for the average female it was 75.5.[16] And birth itself had become a process much less hazardous for mother and child alike. Between 1840 and 1900 about 150 of every 1,000 children died in infancy, but by 1950 the figure was down to 30 per 1,000, and in 1974 it was only 16 per 1,000. Maternal morality had declined even more significantly during the same period.[17]

## Institutional security

The pre-industrial environment had heightened human consciousness of insecurity and powerlessness partly because it had lacked effective safeguards against disasters involving property, employment and livelihood. What disease or famine could do to physical health, unchecked by human knowledge or resource, fire, theft or shipwreck could do to the economic well-being of an individual or a family. The social and psychological consequences of powerlessness against this latter crisis made the modern development of insurance, pension schemes, unemployment relief and related welfare institutions as crucial, in the cultural sphere, as were the more spectacular improvements in science and technology and economic growth which seem more obvious concomitants of modernization.

Life assurance provides a useful example. It had originated in England in the seventeenth century, but until the rapid economic expansion of the early industrial age generated a great increase in personal property, it remained little more than an interesting innovation. Then fourteen major companies sprang up in the opening decade of the nineteenth century. Other forms of insurance, including sickness and unemployment benefit schemes run by benevolent societies, began to assume genuine social significance during the same period, and by about 1840 a contemporary historian calculated that perhaps one family in three had some kind of insurance against 'the unexpected death of their natural protectors'.[18] Human rationality, ingenuity and foresight seemed to be fashioning an institutional environment which greatly mitigated symptoms of human insecurity previously considered intractable. In short, there was a definite cultural dimension to the institutional improvement. 'Every person who is at all conversant with the principles of Life Assurance', concluded the first historian of the new industry,

knows how well it is adapted to avert the melancholy consequences of many of the unforeseen evils to which our race is liable; and how much it contributes, even now, to the happiness and prosperity of the whole community. . . .[19]

There is a growing sense in such utterances, evoked and reinforced as improvement followed improvement, of human achievement – of what Bonhoeffer has called 'the autonomy of man and the world'. Modernization was not just producing an environment more comfortable, more secure, more manipulable, than any which had shaped human consciousness in the past, it was also providing rich food for the hubristic side of human nature. The bold but tenuous ideas of the eighteenth-century Enlightenment could have entered no habitat more encouraging.


## THE SECULAR CULTURE

The new urban-industrial environment, with its massive productivity, rising living standards, material comforts and heady triumphs of human knowledge and industry, began to take shape within a generation or so of the Enlightenment. Lip service, at least, would long be paid to the importance of Christianity as the dominant element in European culture, but after the Enlightenment (as Chapter Two has argued) traditional religious assumptions ceased to be normative. Christian Churches found themselves in competition, not just with each other, but with new ideologies and epistemologies which in some cases were not even remotely religious. But if industrialization has decisive cultural consequences in such circumstances, its influence was not what the prophets of Enlightenment secularism might have expected and hoped for. Secularism, with its characteristically anti-religious animus, has survived as one ingredient among many in a pluralistic modern culture, but the modern industrial environment seems quite as apathetic towards attacks on religion as it does to positive religious commitment.

## Secularism

The early industrial age in fact saw a revival of Enlightenment secularism, not among the aristocratic audiences attracted to it a century earlier, but among the masses. In Britain a popular secularist tradition developed in the wake of Tom Paine's *Age of Reason* (1794), and it flourished within working-class communities while ever there were significant expressions of proletarian religiosity to be countered. Secularism, in short, appeared to thrive under circumstances where less obtrusive processes of secularization met with resistance. And Paine's popularization of the once esoteric infidelity of Voltaire, Bayle or Hume was indeed a controversial development. A religious strain in British radicalism, rooted in the myth and history of Cromwell's age and augmented in the eighteenth century by the popular impact of Methodism, would survive to pass on (albeit in diluted form and with fairly superficial results), into the working-class culture which was beginning to take shape in the early nineteenth century.[20]

But if Paine lost supporters by linking the political radicalism of the *Rights of Man* with the religious infidelity of the *Age of Reason*, as a popular ideologue his instincts were faultless. For he offered ideological legitimation to those members of the working classes for whom traditional religiosity, with all its associations of bourgeois or aristocratic hegemony, became increasingly incongruous as the nineteenth century proceeded. Reports by London City Mission workers provided confirmation of this secularist function throughout most of the Victorian era. They tell of unhappy conflicts by missioners with a strong undercurrent of proletarian secularism, Paineite in its blunt invective and bold ribaldry, which evidently symbolized, to its proponents, the estrangement of classes and cultures which at the same time gave the word 'Mission' a grim appropriateness.[21]

Nevertheless, as the wider process of secularization advanced in the mature industrial society, secularism – with its conscious and aggressive rejection of religious beliefs and values – posed far fewer problems for the Churches than did much more general increases of religious ignorance and apathy. Secularism never obsessed the working classes, and in the twentieth century has become a trivial aspect of working-class culture. And although at a more urbane level men like George Jacob Holyoake and Charles Bradlaugh, skilful agitators and journalists both, orchestrated a more or less constant barrage of anti-religious propaganda throughout the Victorian years, their activities were more a nuisance than a major threat to British Christianity. Indeed, in a society preoccupied increasingly with mundane issues and secular modes of thought, campaigners *against* religion were in the curious position of sharing with their opponents a fundamental problem of demonstrating their own relevance!

In the present century secularism has been led by the Rationalist Press Association, founded in 1899, and the Ethical Union of 1896. These have proved resourceful and well-directed pressure-groups, and the 'Thinker's Library' series of the Association, which began publication in 1930, has provided militant secularism with a particularly effective outlet. As early as 1932, for example, the series had sold 300,000 of what an alarmed champion of orthodoxy, C. S. Lewis, called 'a glut of cheap scientific books written on atheistic principles'.[22] In terms of its overall importance in the development of modern culture, however, this kind of secularist campaign has been of only marginal significance. An index of its attraction as a cause in which people have sought active involvement is the fact that the combined membership of the Rationalist Press Association, the Ethical Union and the British Humanist Association (founded in 1963) has never grown beyond a few thousand.

## Scientism

If secularism is one of the least important ingredients of modern secular culture, the impact of science on popular consciousness certainly has been one of the central themes in its evolution. 'Scientism' describes the kind of worldview derived, not from the scientific method as such, but from popular conceptions – and misconceptions – about the nature and efficacy of science. It has two essential characteristics, one epistemological and the other ideological. Epistemologically it rests on the assumption that all realms of being and knowing are accessible to the methods of empirical science, an assumption reflected in practice by the mentality which regards 'scientific proof' as a kind of legitimating incantation for any kind of factual assertion, advertising gimmick or programme of action. Ideologically it involves the tendency to believe or suspect that anything inaccessible to the scientific method is either irrelevant or even illusory. It is in this sense the nemesis of any metaphysical philosophy.

Historically, the epistemological legacy of Newtonian science has exercised an immense influence on the British mind, and indeed on Western thought generally. Ironically, its normative role in the development of scientism has shown little evidence of weakening in the face of the less mechanistic, relativistic epistemology inherent in the Einsteinian assumptions of modern physical science. What a more informed popular understanding of quantum mechanics and relativity theory might mean for human religiosity remains conjectural. But while an increasing specialization of scientific knowledge suggests that in future information about scientific matters will become more, rather than less, hazy and generalized, human dependence on a ubiquitous science-based technology appears likely to sustain the established assumptions and values. For despite recurrent Titanic-type disasters, including the recent threat of 'melt-down' at Harrisburg, Pennsylvania, popular attitudes towards science are bound to be fashioned largely under the influence of the effective and beneficial applications of science without which modern life would break down. The disasters show that scientists, as human beings, are fallible, and perhaps suggest that certain scientific applications may be too risky to continue; conversely, however, they at the same time reinforce awareness of the fundamental dependence of modern communities and nations on the knowledge and skill of scientific experts who perform modern wonders in mysterious scientific ways. Popular scientism, in short, seems an ineradicable cultural feature of an advanced technological society.

The intimate relationship between science and technology was symbolized in the early stages of the modernization process in Britain when the foundation charter of the Royal Society explicitly linked the pursuit of 'knowledge of natural things' with 'useful arts', including manufactures, engineering and invention.[23] And however close were the actual links between the two during the early industrial age, the general consensus was that they were crucial. In his 1835 treatise *On the Economy of Machinery and Manufactures* Charles Babbage not only argued that the rapid economic growth of the previous half-century had depended on the practical application of scientific discoveries, but insisted that, 'as we advance in the career of improvement, every step requires, for its success, that this connexion should be rendered more intimate'.[24] Such was the conventional wisdom. Its cultural corollaries were a feeling of indebtedness to 'science' for the benefits of material progress, and a growing tendency to regard scientific knowledge and scientific principles as somehow surer, more incontrovertible, than any others. The Newtonian revolution had inaugurated a new era, one in which the methods and discoveries of science had become the 'true foundation' upon which, in the words of Sir Lyon Playfair, the Victorian scientist-turned-politician, 'the superstructure of modern civilization is built'.[25]

By the early Victorian era science had begun to exercise a normative influence on consciousness.[26] Even John Henry Newman, for all his profound misgivings about 'modern' tendencies in almost all their manifestations, could not escape the epistemological imperialism of

57

science, and Christian apologetics in general became increasingly preoccupied with the value of showing that Biblical claims or theological assumptions were scientifically demonstrable or at least plausible. Newman himself, for example, wanted to insist that Christianity was true 'in the sense in which the general facts and the law of the fall of a stone to the earth is true . . . .'[27] Such analogies were inevitable, granted the immense prestige and importance of science in the emerging modern culture; as was the protracted love-hate relationship between theologians and scientific thought which continues, somewhat abated, today.

At a theological and philosophical level, of course, the relationship between science and religion was not a question of 'scientism', but an intellectual debate which has produced some of the most subtle and perceptive examples of modern thought, as well as many of the most passionate, obdurate and facile. In the Victorian period it was a debate often initiated by scientists themselves, or by philosophers speaking on behalf of science. Their motivation was to undermine or modify religious beliefs considered prejudicial to the assimilation of scientific knowledge. Thomas Huxley, the great Victorian apologist for Britain's growing scientific community, frequently adopted aggressively counter-religious positions for precisely this reason. But in the twentieth century the scientific community – now entrenched in the mainstream of national life – has rarely bothered to attack religion, nor have individual scientists often made personal loss of faith an occasion for anti-religious propaganda. Indeed, even in the heat of the Victorian crisis over Darwinism there was something coldly matter-of-fact about Charles Darwin's recollection of the origins of his own agnosticism. Disbelief, he remembered, 'crept over me at a very slow rate, but was at last complete. The rate was so slow that I felt no distress, and have never since doubted even for a single second that my conclusion was correct'.[28]

By no means all scientists shared Darwin's experience of loss of faith. Some professed to find Christian faith through a teleological view of scientific evidence, others found in their scientific knowledge no occasion for either doubt or disbelief. Scientific thought and activity, in other words, was not in itself a direct cause of secularization. It was involved in the process through two important secondary effects. First, it prompted theological responses from Christian intellectuals fascinated by the challenge of integrating science and faith, and the primary tendency of such responses was towards the secularization of theology. This subject will be examined further in Chapter Six, where the discussion focuses on attempts by the churches to come to terms with the secularized 'world' of the industrial age. Secondly, science influenced secularization through the impact of 'scientism' on popular consciousness, for the notion that science and religion are incompatible has been one of the most obvious features of 'scientism'. And even where this counter-religious feature has been absent, popular culture in a world dominated by science and technology has grown indifferent to metaphysical speculation.

The secularization of theology has been of secondary and derivative importance compared with this latter relationship between science and popular culture. Not the views of scientists or theologians *per se*, but the semi-informed, partial, simplistic perceptions of such views – perceptions mediated to the general public through impressionistic journalism, polemical literature, manipulative advertising, or simply through the innumerable experiences of life in an environment dominated by applied science – these are the things which have made 'scientism' a powerful solvent of popular religiosity. It matters not that popular perception never does justice to the sublime insights or precise accommodations of purist theology, and never grasps fully the strict limits of the scientific method as a source of knowledge, for in a modern mass culture the 'conventional wisdom', however distorted, has been the decisive arena of cultural secularization.

Theologians versed in the debates about science and religion have learned to eschew the kind of 'gaps' religiosity which, in this study, is being equated with the outlook of ordinary believers. But popular religion bore to theology the kind of relationship which scientism bore to science. There was profound and – for the effectiveness of the Churches in the modern world – ominous truth in the pungent observations on Christianity which Leslie Stephen published in 1873. 'A religion to be of any value', he wrote in 'Religion as a Fine Art',

must retain a grasp upon the great mass of mankind and the mass are hopelessly vulgar and prosaic. The ordinary Briton persists in thinking that the words 'I believe' are to be interpreted in the same sense in a creed or a scientific statement. His appetite wants something more than 'theosophic moonshine'. He expects that messages from the undiscovered country, whence no traveller returns, should be as authentic as those which Columbus brought from America. He wants to draw aside the mystery by which our little lives are bounded, and to know whether there is, in fact, a beyond and a hereafter. . . . He is so inquisitive that he insists upon knowing whether the word 'God' is to be applied to a being who will interfere, more or less, with his life, or is merely a philosophical circumlocution for the unvarying order of nature.[29]

There is a telling irony in this description of the 'vulgar and prosaic' concerns of popular Christianity, for the viewpoint described is substantially that of the traditional Christian creeds. To the 'ordinary

Briton', in short, religion was nothing if not a revelation of supernatural knowledge, a mediation of supernatural power. Either it was something which would 'interfere, more or less', with human life, or it was not; and the person beginning to suspect the latter was firmly on the path to apathy or unbelief.

A proliferation of technological skills, scientific knowledge, and evidence of human mastery over nature had obvious implications for such 'gaps' religiosity. 'A God who is not allowed even to make a fly or launch a thunderbolt', Stephen pointed out, 'will be worshipped in strains widely different from those which celebrated the Ruler who clothed the horse's neck with thunder, and whose voice shook the wilderness'.[30] This was the crux of cultural secularization, for here the traditional congruity between 'religious' and 'secular' modes of thought broke down. A year after Stephen's essay the intellectual Matthew Arnold could assure his daughter that 'the common anthropomorphic ideas of God and the reliance on miracles must and will inevitably pass away', and could argue that in the process nothing 'desirable or necessary' would be lost.[31] But he was wrong, at least as far as the latter argument applied to traditional British Christianity. A God who was neither personal nor supernatural simply held no meaning within the traditional religious culture, and for this reason a 'modern' or 'liberal' theology portraying such a Being would itself become just another vehicle for secularization.

Indeed, as far as popular Christianity was concerned, Arnold came much closer to the relationship between scientism and religious belief when, in his famous poem 'Dover Beach', he evoked the 'melancholy, long, withdrawing roar' of the Sea of Faith before the 'night-wind' of modernity.[32] Which is not to confuse scientism with secularism. Scientism does not produce conscious opposition to religion, or at least does not commonly do so. It is an outlook, an orientation of the mind, and it challenges religious beliefs and values not chiefly by contradicting them, but rather by fashioning a type of consciousness which leaves little place for religiosity. This anti-metaphysical orientation has, from time to time, found a respectable philosophical mooring in some elaboration of modern empiricism, most notably, perhaps, in the logical positivism of the 1930s. Modern linguistic analysis, too, has gone beyond traditional scepticism or atheism to the point of arguing that questions (or statements) of a metaphysical kind are simply meaningless; yet the fact remains that it is to scientism rather than systematic philosophy that popular religious apathy must be traced.

In a classic statement of the scientism-secularization link, Sir James

Stephen, the eminent Victorian jurist, wrote as long ago as 1884 that:

If human life is in the course of being fully described by science I do not see what materials there are for any religion, or, indeed, what would be the use of one, or why it is wanted. You can get on very well without one, for though the view of life which science is opening up to us gives us nothing to worship, it gives us an infinite number of things to enjoy. . . .[33]

In the final quarter of the twentieth century, the view of life which science is opening up also gives us plenty to worry about! But modern pessimism, no less than nineteenth-century optimism and hedonism, reflects that assumption of the 'autonomy of man and the world' which always has been the basic link between the popularization of science and the growth of secularization.

## The secular way of death

There can be no better exemplification of the link between the material and cognitive environment of modern life, on the one hand, and secularization on the other, than the marked changes evident over time in attitudes to death and mourning. As already noted, among the most profound 'improvements' in the circumstances of British life during the transition to modern industrial culture were the increased longevity and more effective controls over illness and pain which accompanied advances in medicine, sanitation and diet. The recurrent human crises of birth and death took on new meanings, evoked new attitudes, prompted new kinds of psychological adjustment. In the modern world, as Magnus Pyke has put it,

Individuals no longer feel themselves to be subject to the sport and caprice of gods or devils or the evil eye. No longer do they feel that out of the blue and all of a sudden in the full prime of their manhood they may be struck down by a fever which they can do nothing to avoid or resist. It is true that modern middle-aged men may be carried off by lung cancer or coronary heart disease, but these men also know that when they work, eat and smoke too much – or, for that matter, travel too fast or too often in sports-cars – they run a risk by doing so. The universe is a different place for modern men because, for them, it is at least in part under their own control; for their ancestors it was a place of fearful and unmanageable things.[34]

The kind of primeval terror released by the horror word 'cancer' ought not to be minimized but the fact of enormous changes in attitudes to death can scarcely be disputed.

In the pre-industrial age, when early death was a normal occurrence, when disease and pain never were far away, when the causes of ill-health remained almost totally beyond human understanding or control, coping with death was a central issue in cultural and social life.

It had to be faced openly, candidly. Christian belief and ritual served as the major mechanism in this essential adjustment, for a firm acceptance of immortality meant that death could be accepted as much as a beginning as it was an end. In a society in which, as the sixteenth-century *Book of Common Prayer* intoned, 'In the midst of life we are in death', religious consciousness thus received a constant, powerful reinforcement. But in contrast, in the midst of modern life death has become a relative stranger – an intruder whose presence, when it cannot studiously be ignored, causes confusion and embarrassment as well as trauma.

Sociological as well as medical developments have helped create this circumstance, for the decline of the extended family as a residential community has insulated many children and young adults from direct contact with the dead or dying, and the institutionalization of terminal or geriatric patients has reinforced a modern unfamiliarity with death. In consequence, as Geoffrey Gorer pointed out more than a decade ago, the modern response to death combines callousness and squeamishness.[35] Aquainted with the impersonal, 'phoney' phenomenon of death on television, and living in a society conditioned to regard death and mourning as private matters, people react to the abstract idea of death with a kind of indifference which would have been incongruous in an earlier age. Confronted with death as a personal crisis, the same people seem able to do little but retreat squeamishly into euphemism. There has emerged a cultural conspiracy of silence on the subject – a tendency to treat it as indelicate and unmentionable – which leaves death in the same kind of position in modern consciousness as that reserved by the Victorians for that other biological reality, human sexuality.

Admittedly, no manipulation of demographic data seems likely, in the foreseeable future, to evade the truth that 'one out of one dies', and for this reason the fact of death remains the great, inescapable reminder of human powerlessness and insecurity. The argument will return at a later stage to the idea that mortality sets firm limits on secularization. Yet it remains equally true that changing perceptions of death and physical suffering have contributed to the secularization process, for such perceptions have been bound up always with the role of religion in a culture. Indeed, the stage seems to have been reached where the crisis of mortality no longer has much power to evoke genuinely 'religious' responses. 'I'm peculiar, I believe in the New Testament', a recently-widowed Midlands woman told her vicar in the early 1960s, thanking him for offering her Christian consolation in her bereavement.[36] At the end of his survey, Gorer, who reported the conversation, agreed with the woman's assessment of the role of religion in the modern adjustment to death and mourning. He concluded his impressive sample study convinced 'that the majority of British people are today without adequate guidance as to how to treat death and bereavement and without social help in living through the inevitable responses in human beings to the death of someone whom they have loved'.[37] So much had secularization blunted the force of this ultimate 'breaking-point' – at least as an occasion for religiosity – that Gorer identified a need for 'social inventions which will provide secular mourning rituals for the bereaved, their kin and their friends and neighbours'.[38]

## Rationality

Fundamental to the argument of this chapter is the idea that cultural movements and ideological systems can become potent agents of secularization without involving conscious 'secularism', or indeed without having any direct bearing on the truth or falsity of religious faith. Any cultural development tending to preoccupy people with ideas, interests and knowledge bereft of supernatural, metaphysical, other-worldly assumptions, tends inevitably towards secularization. Thus to the extent that modern Britain has become a society preoccupied with technical skills, scientific knowledge, mundane goals and humanistic values, the Christian religion has become epiphenomenal within it; and this is true despite the fact that the skills, knowledge, goals and values in question are not, in most cases, inherently counter-religious. In historical perspective, the kind of world now shaped by the dictates of science, technology and bureaucracy has carried 'this-worldly rationality' beyond the point where, in the period Weber analysed, it interacted positively with Protestant asceticism, to the point where any metaphysical thought is stultified by it.

Weber was of course aware of this historical development. 'Rationality', he conceded, has become part of the essential logic of modern society: part of the 'fate of our times'. Through the rationalization of economic and social structures in urban–industrial life, the growing dependence on bureaucracy as an organizing principle, the substitution of artificial rhythms and realities for a once-direct and obvious dependence on nature – through these inescapable features of modernity – a social order has emerged in which 'there are no mysterious incalculable forces that come into play', in which 'one can, in principle, master all things by calculation'.[39] Rational organization, Alex Inkeles has argued in an important article on modernization, is a 'hidden persuader' , a 'silent and unobserved teacher' of the kinds of attitudes, values and ways of acting designated as 'modern'.[40] Religion's crisis of plausibility in modern culture, precisely because it reflects more or less unconscious, reflexive orientations of the mind rather than specific intellectual doubts, has more to do with this generalized, subtle assumption of rationality' than with any other aspect of the modern world.

Aldous Huxley's 'Elinor Quales', of *Point Counter Point*, who found religious ideas and motives 'oddly incomprehensible', is a paradigm of modern areligious rationality. Able to admire genuine religiosity for its sincerity, she felt that 'it was all rather absurd and superfluous', for

she never remembered a time, even in her childhood, when she seriously believed what people told her about the other world and its inhabitants. The other world bored her; she was interested only in this. . . . Religion and, along with religion, all transcendental morality, all metaphysical speculation seemed to her nonsensical in precisely the same way as the smell of Gorgonzola seemed to her disgusting. There was no getting behind the immediate experience.[41]

The immediate experience was itself complex, something shaped by the subtle realities of life in a modern environment, and the historian of secularization can only generalize about the specific relationship between this environment and religion's crisis of plausibility.

Clearly, however, an important aspect of the relationship has to do with the fact that the modern world is artificial rather than natural. It is a habitat fashioned by the human species for itself, autonomous (in many respects) from non-human influences. A hallmark of modernity is enhanced consciousness of human responsibility. Human self-confidence might wane, but the modern environment seems likely to remain hostile to traditional religious consciousness while ever optimists and pessimists alike share this historically novel sense of human responsibility. In John F. Kennedy's much-quoted words: 'Man holds in his mortal hands the power to destroy all forms of human poverty and all forms of human life.' Either way, the traditional 'salvationism' which seeks supernatural aid at the limits of human knowledge and power is denied authenticity. The old orthodoxy may be true, but in a modern environment it is certainly less plausible than ever before.

For the time is past, in modern societies, when *homo sapiens* was obliged, like other species, to live in direct and immediate harmony with the rhythms of nature, and to adjust both consciousness and behaviour to the unpredictability, bounty and scarcity of the natural world. Modern culture has been fashioned by a different set of adjustments. The modern child is brought up, in many cases, without a feeling of dependence on the tides or the seasons, the vagaries of weather, wind and harvest. The modern equivalents are almost exclusively matters of human contrivance: television programmes and railway timetables, institutionalized forms of entertainment, and the spectacle of an adult world dominated by the artificial rhythms of stock market, interest rates, wages policies, inflation and unemployment. The crises, failures and disasters of such an environment may, potentially, exceed those associated with what insurance brokers and religious believers still call 'acts of God', yet they are so patently human failures, aberrations in an artificial system, that they evoke no obvious metaphysical response or supernatural explanation.

The work processes of the modern age, rooted in the artificiality and man-made complexity of the production line and the machine, are the central pillars of its this-worldly rationality and its consciousness (or false consciousness) of autonomy. 'The factory can be a school – a school for modernization', Inkles has remarked, echoing the perception expressed a century earlier in Andrew Ure's evocative phrase, 'the moral economy of the factory'.[42] Apart from the obvious effects on consciousness of the tyranny of the clock and the discipline of the machine, the structural differentiation of work processes played a profound role in this education of the modern mind. As Adam Smith's famous example from the pin-making industry illustrated, the process of industrialization involved the progressive breaking-down of an overall manufacturing enterprise (such as making a pin), into a number of specialized tasks. While one workman responsible for the total process could not hope to produce more than twenty pins in a day, and might in fact produce far fewer, ten workman, by differentiating the apparently simple task of pin-making into a series of distinct operations, could produce 48,000 pins per day – a rate of almost 5,000 per man per day! This principle became a basic premise of industrial organization in the factory, and later on the assembly line. The individual worker no longer produced any complete item, but exercised a highly specialized function significant only as part of a vast, rationalized system of production.

Alienation, as Marx emphasised, was one obvious symptom of this modern, rationalized approach to work. Another symptom – more important in the present context – was the tendency for the specialization of roles and competences in the society (at all levels of work and activity), to increase the dependence of individuals on the overall system. The skilled professional, manager or entrepreneur is highly rewarded in the complex, artificial world of contemporary industrial society: outside it he would be relatively powerless, incompetent, bewildered. Inevitably, then, his consciousness, outlook and values take shape around the comfortable, controlled, limited and artificial realities of mundane existence. There is an arresting theological corollary to this fact. If the naturalness of religious consciousness in a pre-modern environment reflected the inescapable need for some kind of metaphysical element in the adjustment of consciousness to perceived reality, the seeming incongruity of religiosity in the modern world reflects the ruling imperative to find meaning and security in the very rationality through which humanity makes its claim to mastery. If, in other words, modernity means that mankind has 'come of age',[43] then now, as never before, the Christian dictum that one must be 'as a little child' to enter the Kingdom of God presupposes for Christianity a sub-cultural role in a world which finds metaphysics of any variety immature and implausible.

To avoid becoming itself secularized in such an environment, and at the same time to have an impact on its contemporary 'world', the modern Church must accept a prophetic relationship with the dominant culture. It must elaborate an effective critique of modern secular rationality. It must be as much counter-cultural as it is, inescapably, sub-cultural. The world may never be greatly influenced, but there will be accompanying counter-cultural movements supportive in the diagnosis of contemporary ills, if not in the kinds of remedies advocated. Indeed, the greatest of the modern prophets are at present secular in outlook, even although the triumph of their ideas would represent an emphatic reversal of modern secularization. Herbert Marcuse is a case in point. 'Industrial society', he has argued,

possesses the instrumentalities for transforming the metaphysical into the physical, the inner into the outer, the adventures of the mind into adventures of technology. The terrible phrases (and realities of) 'engineers of the soul', 'head shrinkers', 'scientific management', 'science of consumption', epitomize (in a miserable form) the progressive rationalization of the irrational, of the 'spiritual' – the denial of the idealistic culture.[44]

But however acute their message, however incisive their critique, it takes a convulsion in the mainstream culture before prophets cease to be mere voices crying in a wilderness. And it is perhaps an index of the extent to which supernatural religion had been relegated to the edges of modern consciousness that even Marcuse, for all his deep misgivings about the sterile rationality of modern Western culture, feels sufficiently uneasy about the traditionally taken-for-granted notion of the 'spiritual' to italicize the word in a stylized admission of diffidence.

# NOTES

1. Murphy, H. R. (1955), p. 816.
2. Briggs, A. (1959).
3. Perkin, H. (1969), p. 5.
4. Ibid.
5. Ibid.
6. Oswald, J. (1768), pp. 366-9.
7. Thomas, K. (1973), p. 6.
8. Ibid.
9. Ibid., p. 7.
10. Ibid., pp. 7-10.
11. Ibid., p. 15.
12. Ibid., p. 20.
13. See, for example, Deane, P. and Cole, W. A. (1962), or Mitchell, B. R. and Deane, P. (1962) for detailed statistical analysis of these trends.
14. Smith, Adam (1909), p. 34.
15. See, for example, Eversley, D. C. (1967).
16. Thomas, K. (1973), p. 6; Thompson, E. J. (1976), p. 135.
17. Thompson, E. J. (1976), p. 135.
18. St Clair, W. (1840), p. v.
19. Ibid., p. iv.
20. For a variety of perspectives on this complex theme see: Lacqueur, T. W. (1976), Royle, E. (1971), Semmel, B. (1974), Thompson, E. P. (1968) and Ward, W. R. (1972).
21. I owe this information to Robert Currie, who has worked on the L.C.M. records.
22. Whyte, A. G. (1949), p. 77.
23. Mathias, P. (1972), p. 61.
24. Babbage, C. (1835), p. 379.
25. 'Science and Technology as Sources of National Power', in Basalla, G., Coleman, W. and Kargon, R. H. (1970), p. 82.
26. See Cannon, W. F. (1964).
27. Quoted by Cannon, W. F. (1964), p. 496.
28. Greene, J. C. (1963), p. 14.
29. Stephen, L. (1873), p. 95-6.
30. Ibid.
31. Arnold, M. (1895), p. 120.
32. The poem was published in 1867.
33. *Nineteenth Century*, lxxxviii (June 1884), p. 917.
34. Pyke, M. (1967), p. 18.
35. Toynbee, A. (1968), pp. 122-32.
36. Gorer, G. (1965), p. 42.
37. Ibid., p. 110.
38. Ibid., p. 116.
39. Gerth, H. H. and Mills, C. W. (1946), p. 155.
40. Inkeles, A. (1969), p. 213.
41. Huxley, A. (1928), p. 360.
42. Inkeles, A. (1969), p. 213.
43. Bonhoeffer, D. (1953), p. 146.
44. Marcuse, H. (1968), p. 234.

# CHAPTER FOUR

# The evolution of a secular society

However much it might improve upon the substance or detail of the preceding analysis, a study of the emergence of a modern secular culture can describe only partially the difficulties which the modern Churches face in their contemporary 'world'. For religion is a social phenomenon as well as a matter of human consciousness and culture, and if beliefs and values are the primary aspects of religious commitment they are neither acquired nor maintained in isolation of the social environment in which an adherent lives. Religious experiences are to a significant extent shared experiences, involving people as social groups and not simply as individuals; and they are at the same time largely recurrent experiences, prompting repetitive responses. Religion does not endure, therefore, simply as a series of unstructured, unsystematic, spontaneous perceptions and experiences of the supernatural. Recurrent responses become ritualized. Beliefs and assumptions are, in time, systematized into dogma. Group responses are institutionalized. Religious organizations and functionaries appear, and, in one form or another, questions about property, power and preferment invade the province of simple faith and pure spirituality.

This scenario is familiar to sociologists of religion as a 'routinization of charisma', a model of religious development which implies that institutional and organizational forms are not just secondary phenomena, but also very often instruments stultifying the free and total expression of an original religious consciousness. Historically, however, the evolution of religious movements rarely falls so neatly into patterns which imply that the faith is primary and its social expressions derivative. Indeed, certain scholars, including such giants as Emile Durkheim and Karl Marx, have argued that it is the religious consciousness itself which is derivative. To Durkheim religion seemed to reflect a basic communal imperative for reaffirming social cohesion by cultural means. To Marx it seemed that religious beliefs and values evolved as part of the cultural and institutional superstructure shaped ultimately by the modes and relations of production inherent in the dominant economic system of a society.

These are extreme views. But it is clear that a religious movement, however uncompromising its theology, however intense the spirituality of its adherents, is caught up in the social realities of the wider world simply by virtue of the fact that those adherents, as long as they live, must share the mundane, earthly dictates arising from the inescapable needs of shelter, food, companionship and security. By the same logic, religious organizations, functionaries and practices straddle the boundary between the sacred and the profane, and serve the needs and aspirations of human participants in both areas. Social aspects of religion therefore provide clear and early evidence of changes in the relationship between 'church' and 'world'. It follows that a massive intensification of religious consciousness, such as the Methodist revival of the eighteenth century, is at the same time a massive social unheaval, and leads subsequently to the development of powerful new institutions and organizations in the wider society. Equally, however, an institutional decline of religion, or a tendency for religious institutions to be adapted to increasingly mundane purposes, is a fairly reliable barometer of cultural secularization.

This chapter takes the argument further. The social aspect of religion can be an initiator, not just a barometer of change in the role of religion in a society. Chapter Three has looked at the human and material environment in which cultural changes associated with modernization took place in Britain. Now the study turns to patterns of social structure developing in this environment, especially the dramatic transformation from largely rural to predominantly urban settlement patterns, the disappearance of traditional community life, the rise of class structures as primary social barriers, and changes in modes of welfare, social control, education, recreation and family life since the Industrial Revolution. While profound changes in Western intellectual and material culture created a modern crisis of religious plausibility, these social and institutional changes faced the British Churches with a different, more immediate, kind of challenge. Secularization was operating at more than one level, advancing in different ways at different speeds.

## THE HISTORICAL BACKGROUND

Reformation, spoliation, civil war defeat and Cromwellian eclipse, uneasy 'Restoration' and the need, a generation later, to concede a measure of religious toleration to sectarian opponents – these were the unhappy memories of the eighteenth-century Church of England. Yet on the eve of Britain's industrialization and modernization Anglicanism remained a powerful element in the political, social and legal structures of the society. Scotland, of course, was exempt from its influence; in Ireland, and in Wales to a lesser extent, the religious Establishment had more form than substance; and in many English parishes, especially in the under-staffed, inadequately endowed dioceses of the West Country, the North and West Midlands and northern counties, institutional decay and clerical negligence had already seriously weakened whatever hold Christianity had managed to obtain over the hearts and minds of local communities.[1] These are crucial qualifications. But the fact remains that the bulk of the British population lived in the southern and eastern areas of England, where the Church was relatively strong, and that even where it was not well-equipped for a pastoral or spiritual role, Anglicanism could continue to exercise vital social, legal and political functions in a locality or region.

The Church of England parochial system remained the basic unit of local administration and social welfare; the Church dominated education, from the parochial elementary schools to the ancient universities; its bishops sat in the House of Lords, and by the early nineteenth century some two thousand of its lower clergy sat as Justices on what in practical terms was often a more important institution, a County Bench of magistrates. Its wealth as a landowning institution was immense and conspicuous, and landed wealth still carried enormous informal 'influence' in the early industrial age. Inevitably, in such circumstances Holy Orders offered professional as well as vocational inducements; indeed, until the ecclesiastical changes of the 1830s the Church could be considered more likely than either the legal profession or the armed services to provide the kind of remuneration, status and prospects of advancement attractive to the sons of the gentry.

These are fairly familiar details, but their significance in the history of secularization requires some elaboration. For the Church of England, at least in the early stages of Britain's industrialization and modernization, was in a position of false security. Its inherited structural advantages often obscured mounting problems of maintaining the credibility of its specifically 'religious' services, and at the same time its immense social prestige and influence made this 'religious' failure, even when it was observed, seem less serious than it would appear in retrospect. The development of Anglicanism in the period of early industrialization was, in short, profoundly ambiguous. Its spiritual influence declined, its religious services were neglected more than ever before, yet at the same time social, economic and political changes in the wider society were raising the *social* pre-eminence of the Church of England to a level unparalleled since before the Civil War.

The figures are incomplete, but unequivocal. The population of England and Wales rose from around six million in 1740 to almost 18 million by the middle of the nineteenth century, but the number of Anglican clergy and churches remained almost stationary, and their deployment became increasingly ineffective as the demographic centre of gravity shifted from the rural heartland of the South-East towards the urban and industrial centres of the Midlands and the North. For Anglican practice to have kept up with population growth under such circumstances would have been quite impossible. Indeed, what evidence there is suggests that the decline was absolute, not simply relative to the rate of demographic expansion. A sample of Oxford diocesan parishes during the period between 1738 and 1802, for example, shows an actual fall from 911 communicants to only 682. The 25 per cent decline may not have been typical. The average may have been better – or worse. But it is certain that in an expanding society Anglicanism had lost touch, as a religious institution, with very large sections of the population.[2]

Despite flagging Anglican 'religiosity', however, the social position of the Church in the early nineteenth century was, in certain important respects, stronger than it had been a century earlier. In many parts of the country tithe commutation for land had increased the wealth and status of the clergy,[3] and even where no such windfall had been possible, clergy had found themselves drawn towards the circles of local authority and genteel influence. This had happened as the landed interest, its traditional ascendancy threatened by the growth of commerce and the beginnings of industrialization, had become increasingly attracted to the institutional resources and cultural authority which still survived in church and rectory. A conservative alliance of squire and parson, with the squirarchy the dominant partner, thus became a distinctive feature of English life on the eve of the Industrial Revolution. And if the new version of establishment theory bound Anglicanism rather too closely to the fortunes of a passing socio-political elite, in the short term it certainly enhanced the position of the Church as a social institution.

Complacency thus survived amidst evidence of pastoral neglect and public disenchantment. The need for Church reform, the urgency with which the minority Evangelical Party pursued new forms of pastoral care and conversionist activity, and the challenge of Methodism, Dissent and irreligion were alike ignored, or neglected, by the Church as a whole until the crisis years of the 1830s. Indeed, complacency about apparent 'spiritual' turpitude sometimes arose quite explicitly from assumptions that the Church's primary responsibilities were social, not 'religious'. In this important sense it can be argued that Anglicanism's strength, derived largely from its secular functions, actually hastened its secularization as a religious culture. For as long as the Church upheld the institutions and values of English landed society – while it reinforced and symbolized the interlocking relationships of deference and paternalism which gave the so-called *dependency system* its cohesion – many of its influential leaders and lay supporters would be content to ignore evidence of cultural secularization.

There was, moreover, another way in which the social and political authority inherited by the early nineteenth-century Church of England helped to shape the secularization process. If Anglicanism was a ruling-class institution, an elitest ideology, it followed that opposition to traditional systems of authority would assume a religious dimension. Because the Church defended not just ancient religious truths but also entrenched social values and political realities, 'Anglican' sympathies spread well beyond the ranks of essentially 'religious' conformists. And obversely, people with essentially 'religious' objections to the Established Church very easily found themselves caught up in wider social and political conflicts. Questions of motivation doubtless were impossibly blurred in individual cases, but it is clear that at the level of political and social alignments a basic feature of nineteenth-century society was that structural changes of a thoroughly secular kind advanced under the guise of campaigns for (and against) religious equality.

It had been the rise of Protestant Nonconformity which had completed the scenerio in which religious conflict could mirror the wider tensions and confrontations of the industrializing society. The roots of the nineteenth-century 'Church' – 'chapel' hostilities went back to the sixteenth and seventeenth centuries, when the Elizabethan Settlement had failed to impose genuine religious uniformity on Britain. The Civil War and its aftermath had merely institutionalized these older differences, and if the Old Dissent of the period before 1700 never had effectively challenged the numerical supremacy of the Church of England, it had kept alive the idea of religious nonconformity. The stage had been set for the emergence, in the first half of the eighteenth century, of movements strong enough to carry British Christianity towards genuine religious pluralism.

Amidst new circumstances of religious toleration, Hanoverian stability and early signs of economic and demographic 'revolution', Methodism had begun to grow rapidly. Within John Wesley's own lifetime it had become a spectacular social and religious movement, and under its influence Baptist and Congregationalist elements of the Old Dissent had acquired the 'methodistical' qualities of conversionist zeal and itinerant evangelism. Together these forces had produced a new, popular evangelicalism able to exploit aspects of early industrial society with which Anglicanism could not, or would not, cope. At first it has had no deep, anti-Establishment animus. Even the New Dissent, for all its legacy of historical conflict, had adopted, in practice, the classical Wesleyan posture of *ecclesiola in ecclesia*, content to multiply voluntary associations whose only indictment of the somewhat formalistic State Church had been their unbounded religious 'enthusiasm'.

In the long run, however, conflict inevitably had become the primary mode of 'Church' – 'chapel' relations. Because the social orientation of Anglicanism had been monopolistic and prescriptive, the voluntarism of the newer movements had been seen, with some justification, as subversive. By the late 1780s the Church had begun, more or less systematically, to take a hard line against the Methodists; and Methodism, however much its conservative leaders resisted the trend, had been forced gradually to adopt the kind of independent social attitudes and ecclesiastical postures which had long given a socio-political dimension to English Dissent. Throughout the period from the repeal of the Test and Corporation Acts in 1828 to the era of ecumenical fraternity after World War I, tension and conflict between Anglicanism and Dissent – 'Church' and 'chapel' – became, and remained, the primary determinant of the role and significance of religion in public life. Methodism engaged less heatedly in anti-Establishment politics than did most of the older Nonconformist bodies, and it would of course be quite wrong to see conflict as the only context for interpreting nineteenth-century English and Welsh religious history. Much energy, on either side, was directed towards common objectives. There were always instances of co-operation, of enterprises shared, of overlapping allegiances and of membership transfers. Conflict, however, was the norm. And in the social history of secularization its significance requires special examination.

Had Britain been a one-church society, secularization could have proceeded more or less unobtrusively, sapping the strength of religious institutions gradually as social concerns and political alignments shifted in ways which required neither traditional religious legitimations nor the skills or resources of traditional religious functionaries. Secular education schemes, welfare agencies administered by the State, modes of dispensing public information and running local society without recourse to the ancient parochial system – such 'modern' developments, emerging gradually, would gradually have undermined the social significance and structural importance of organized religion. In practice, however, while such processes of institutional secularization *did* proceed apace in the period from about 1830 to 1914, religion enjoyed continuing social prominence because, fortuitously, the conflicts, tensions and political alignments precipitated during Britain's transition to urban society and liberal democracy coincided precisely with inherited religious confrontations between 'Church' and 'chapel'.

In *The Making of Victorian England*, perhaps the best-known general survey of the Victorian era, G. Kitson Clark rightly stressed the importance of religious alignments in the secular politics of the period between the First Reform Bill and the First World War. Religion, he wrote, 'had received so political a shape, or politics so religious a shape, that it was for many people almost impossible to separate the two'. Church-chapel conflict at times became a secular political obsession, and politicians and voters alike often appear to have 'referred everything back to it'.[4] But if the general or political history of Victorian society can ill-afford to ignore the social reality of religion, in a history of secularization it is important to recognize the partial and tenuous character of this 'religious' contribution. For while the churches as social organizations were continuing to thrive, at least among certain social classes, the future of British Christianity was being threatened by cultural developments antithetical to the *a priori* plausibility of religious beliefs and values. The former process obscured the seriousness of the latter.

At least over the short term, political involvements unquestionably strengthen the positions of 'Church' and 'chapel' alike. In the present context examples must suffice, but the details have become increasingly familiar in recent years.[5] The great 'religious revivals' of 1859-60, in which all major British Churches shared, coincided with the peak of liberal political agitation against compulsory Church Rates, an agitation which inevitably precipitated strenuous conservative efforts to defend this religious symbol of ancient privilege. Both parties to the ensuing political and electoral conflict exploited organized religion as the best available infrastructure for constituency politics. Under the co-ordination of the Liberation Society, Nonconformity's most powerful pressure group, local chapels became centres of Liberal propaganda, agitation and petitioning; and in response, Tory politicians, Anglican clergymen and specially formed Church Defence Associations used the parochial system of the Church of England to counter the Liberal strategy of exploiting the Church Rates issue for secular political ends. The result, of course, was not simply the eventual disappearance of Church Rates as compulsory levies: involvement in the secular battle gave Anglicans and Nonconformists a social and political *raison d'être*. No one would argue that religious revivals were nothing more than political phenomena, but it was no accident that the flooding of 'Church' and 'chapel' membership rolls in 1859-60, and on other comparable occasions, coincided with the large-scale mobilization of English and Welsh society around ostensibly religious issues, slogans and organizations.

The Churches, as social organizations, could defy the more subterranean processes of cultural secularization as long as they retained such political and social utility. The last great period of religious fervour in the Victorian and Edwardian eras – the 'revivals' of 1904–05 – coincided in England and Wales with the final and most intense socio-political conflict to revolve around the differences of 'Church' and 'chapel'. Again it is clear that revivalist fervour was intimately associated with a massive popular campaign against a religious symbol of perceived social privilege: in this case the Tory Education Act of 1902. Political enthusiasm and religious mobilization went hand in hand. As the Welsh historian, K. C. Morgan, has pointed out: 'It required a sophisticated audience indeed to distinguish between the nonconformist minister as revivalist and as sectarian politician'.[6]

If Wales shared the English experience of an Anglican Establishment, in other ways it had more in common with non-English areas of the British Isles. Outside England, the relationship between religion and society often reflected, among other things, the utility of distinctive religious traits as means of expressing a natural resentment against the perceived hegemony of a metropolitan English culture. Welsh religion, for example, was not only influenced by the wider Nonconformist animosities against the Church of England (which until 1920 remained the Established Church in the Principality), but also by a clear identification of nineteenth-century Welsh Nonconformity with a traditional anti-English, nationalistic strain in Welsh consciousness. The chapel community, certainly until the post-1918 period, remained a vital centre of Welsh culture. It served as a focus for Welsh language and Cambrian loyalties, and without doubt its constituent churches benefited as religious organizations from the wider social and cultural importance which this role implied.

A similar kind of analysis is applicable to Presbyterianism in Scotland, to Protestantism in Ulster, and to Catholicism both in Ireland and among Irish immigrant communities in Liverpool, Glasgow, London and other British cities. Catholicism underwent profound renewal in nineteenth-century Ireland, a movement at once abetting and capitalizing upon the rise of Irish nationalism and the growth of political resentment against the English. In Scotland loyalty to Presbyterianism was sustained, in part, by its central role in the affirmation of a separate Scottish identity. And in Ulster, even to the present day, the strength of organized religion must be explained to a considerable extent by its essentially secular, this-worldly function as a symbol and an institutionalization of vital social and cultural differences.

## SECULARIZATION OBSCURED

At least until the 1880s, and (despite early symptoms of organizational decline), with little apparent diminution before the First World War, British religion retained an historical importance among the central institutions of the society. The culture may have been growing more secular, but a variety of social and political factors, aided by the inertial forces of habit and custom, continued to provide social satisfactions within the Churches sufficient, apparently, to attract and retain adherents whose support might otherwise have been lost. Figures on religious practice were not particularly depressing, at least superficially, in the nineteenth and early twentieth centuries. But appearances were deceptive. The fact was that residual social advantages were simply obscuring, temporarily, the impact of cultural secularization.

Patterns of church growth in Britain recently have received very careful analysis.[7] Membership, attendance and related series indicate that in all the major Churches organizational expansion continued to the eve of the First World War. From the early 1880s Nonconformists generally grew more slowly than their constituent populations, while figures on Anglican 'Easter-Day Communicants', Presbyterian membership and the Catholic Church's 'Estimated Catholic Population' showed relative as well as absolute increases. The different series are not strictly comparable, of course. Nonconformist membership represented a higher level of commitment than Anglican Easter Communion, and certainly signified more than 'Estimated

Catholic Population'. When figures on Anglican adult baptisms or Catholic adult conversions are compared with figures on the recruitment, by Nonconformist groups, of adults not previously connected with a chapel community, the growth patterns do exhibit similar trends.[8]

Catholicism must nevertheless be treated separately in a consideration of the growth pattern. If it mirrored common trends, Catholic recruitment certainly was more buoyant than that of any other major religious body as institutional difficulties began to appear. In the present context, however, it is the Protestant pattern which is significant, for in most of Britain it was the Protestant denominations which had been in a position to exploit the kinds of socio-political functions likely to have postponed the institutional impact of secularization. And when the pattern is examined, it is clear that if supportive social and political forces had been operating in favour of organized Protestantism in the Victorian and Edwardian eras, their significance waned with the First World War, lost further ground in the 1930s and during the Second World War, and disappeared more or less completely from about 1960.

Organizational decline, in short, has been uneven. All the Churches lost ground substantially during World War I. The decline was arrested in the 1920s, when even in proportion to the still-growing British population most Churches virtually held their own. But by the early 1930s indices of total membership and membership density (membership as a percentage of adult population), were again in decline. The Second World War exacerbated this trend, and the recovery which followed in the late 1940s and early 1950s was minimal even in comparison with the short-lived upturn after the First World War. Worse was to follow, however. Since 1960 declining membership, attendance, Sunday-school participation, baptisms, confirmations, and numbers of candidates offering themselves for the professional ministry have presented a consistent picture of massive crisis.

In the single decade of the 1960s, for example, Episcopalian 'Easter-Day Communicants' fell by 24.5 per cent in England, 32 per cent in Wales and 12 per cent in Scotland. The Church of Scotland actually ceased to count 'Active Communicants' as early as 1959, but the splinter organization, the United Free Church of Scotland, which maintained the series, saw it decline by 26 per cent in the decade. In England, Presbyterian 'Active Communicants' were 17 per cent fewer in 1970 than they had been ten years earlier. Figures on membership, a more sluggish index, showed a 15 per cent decline in Methodism, a 22 per cent decline in Congregationalism and a 13 per cent decline in Baptist strength in the 1960s. The most recent figures indicate that the 1970s have brought no substantial reversal of this trend, and have seen it accelerate in some Churches. Counter-trends, conspicuous in the growth patterns of certain forms of sectarian Christianity, will be considered in the final section of the study. But as far as the historic Protestant denominations are concerned, twentieth-century religious statistics chart, quite clearly, a path leading – if not towards extinction – then certainly towards the unenviable status of small, residual social organizations.[9]

What can be made of this pattern in a study of secularization? On the surface, at least, the implication seems to be that whatever underlies the decline of religion in modern society has been operating powerfully only since 1914, and with devastating force only since about 1960. But there are good reasons for rejecting so glib an interpretation. First, there is the argument, already discussed, indicating that throughout the Victorian era, and indeed beyond it, religion's inherited social prominence and continuing involvement in mainstream politics masked the impact of cultural secularization because it guaranteed, at least temporarily, the Churches' institutional significance. And secondly, a closer examination of the pre-1914 growth pattern reveals that the roots of the twentieth-century decline stretch back deep into the nineteenth century.

Like any other organization, a Church meets institutional difficulties by changes in strategy, modifications of membership criteria and related measures which tend to obscure, for as long as possible, symptoms of decline. In a recent study entitled *Churches and Churchgoers: Patterns of Church Growth in the British Isles Since 1700*, Robert Currie, Lee Horsley and the present author have distinguished between four different phases in the growth and decline of a religious organization. The first is a *progressive* phase, in which the organization expands rapidly by mobilizing the wider society. The second is a *marginal* phase, in which the responsiveness of the wider society stabilizes, or tends to decline, while the organization maintains its position relative to its constituent population through more efficient membership–retention and enhanced facilities for the recruitment of members' children. The third phase is *recessive*. In it the organization begins to decline as its capacity to recruit 'outsiders' (*allogenous growth*) is reduced markedly, and its reliance on the kind of *autogenous growth* afforded by the recruitment of adherents and members' children begins to deplete these internal constituencies. Finally, the organization enters a *residual* phase. It has virtually no constituency in the wider society, and therefore almost no allogenous growth; mounting demoralization among members seriously reduces both membership-retention and autogenous growth; and the slow net losses of the recessive phase give way to rapid net losses and the prospect of extinction.[10]

When this model is applied to data on British Protestantism in the period since the Evangical Revival of the eighteenth century generated progressive growth in most of the major Protestant traditions, it is clear that the secondary phase of marginal growth began around the beginning of the Victorian era and lasted until the First World War, that the ensuing recessive phase continued until about 1960, and that since 1960 most of the Churches have been caught up in the critical residual phase. The implication is that an analysis of the institutional difficulties of twentieth-century Protestantism must begin with an appreciation of the factors operating in the Victorian era when growth ceased to be progressive and became marginal. The figures may not have looked particularly unhealthy on casual scrutiny. But even contemporary analysts, lacking the hindsight of sociologists who now know that the Victorian Churches were on the brink of massive twentieth-century decline, knew that the growth processes underlying marginal membership increases reflected certain very discouraging trends.

The most critical trend was the mounting failure of religious organizations to maintain earlier levels of recruitment from the wider society, or sections of it. The 'external constituencies' which had supplied allogenous growth were either contracting, becoming less easy to mobilize, or both. In their early days, for example, the Methodist and New Dissenting movements had been able to attract members from the labouring and artisan sections of the population in considerable numbers, but the Victorian working classes were virtually impervious to their influence.[11] Such Churches retained their relative numerical position in the society only by relaxing membership standards to accommodate declining levels of commitment, by improving methods of autogenous growth based on Sunday schools and the religious socialization of members' children, and because they continued to benefit from the formal and informal social pressures favouring public religiosity among the Victorian and early twentieth-century middle classes.

The relaxation of membership standards, like the evolution of new ecclesiastical strategies for exploiting 'internal' Sunday-school and familial constituencies, is a matter of the religious response to secularization: the subject of Part Three of this study. But identifying supportive social factors and, specifically, explaining their decline in the contemporary social environment, is central to any understanding of the secularization of the modern 'world'. In Britain the most important supportive pressures came traditionally from three sources. First there was the age-old heritage, older even than the Christian Church which had inherited it, of religion as communal activity. Secondly, there were the advantages, summarized earlier, of the centrality which religious institutions derived from their implication in mainstream politics. And finally, there were the inertial advantages of a social outlook which equated formal religiosity with social respectability. It follows that to analyse the gradual disintegration of Christianity's historically favourable social environment in Britain is to examine changes in patterns of community, politics and conventions of respectability in the modern society.

## RELIGION, COMMUNITY AND SECULARIZATION

Churches as social organizations are effective only when their own structures mirror those of the societies which they seek to serve. In order to thrive they must adapt themselves to the basic social divisions and settlement patterns of their constituencies. The medieval parochial system provides an obvious example of an ideal structural relationship. The parish developed as a territorial unit encompassing a single, coherent community. It was the primary ecclesiastical entity. In most respects it remained functionally autonomous from its larger diocesan associations which, in turn, were shaped by the territorial, administrative and economic realities of a larger zone encompassing many parochial communities.

The idea of 'community' requires fairly careful definition when it is used in this context. Communal configurations are not the only kinds of human relationships. Indeed, in the typical urban environment of a modern industrial society other configurations have become more common and more important. In searching for an adequate definition it is logical to begin with the traditional territorial community of the village, a largely autonomous, largely exclusive social system which embraced up to 80 per cent of the British population as recently as the early eighteenth century. In the village the individual was dependent on the same group of people, fellow-members of the same community, for almost everything – for livelihood, social status, sociability and recreation, sexual mores and social welfare, education, gossip and religion. Relationships were complex because the individual related at different levels and in different roles to a social group sufficiently limited for personal acquaintance to over-ride formal role relationships. Whereas in the anonymity of modern urban society role relationships between, for example, shop assistant and customer, policeman and citizen, repairman and householder, and even parent and teacher or doctor and patient, have tended to become secondary and impersonal, in a village community they inevitably were personalized by ties of kinship, friendship (or enmity), and a generalized awareness of common, almost familial bonds.

It was to this traditional communal configuration of human society that the territorial parochial system of the Church of England was ideally suited. Just as parochial boundaries had been designed originally to make each parish co-terminus with a self-contained community, so parish organization, institutions and ideals had evolved to fit the social and cultural realties of community life. In an observation which evoked an appropriately familial image of 'community', Robert Southey wrote in 1820 that

Each parish being in itself a little commonwealth, it is easy to conceive that before manufactures were introduced, or where they do not exist, a parish, where the minister and the parochial officers did their duty with activity and zeal, might be almost as well ordered as a private family.[12]

Even in 1820, as the phrase 'before manufactures were introduced' implies, the age of the parochial community was passing into history. Its passing reflected two things. First, during the early industrial age the parochial system had remained an almost static institution in a society rapidly expanding. It was not possible, wrote Richard Yates, whose work on the Church had deeply influenced Southey, 'to view without astonishment and terror the population nearly doubled, and *no further additional* means employed to convey the benefits of the Established Religion to the Minds and Habits of nearly the *additional half* of Inhabitants'.[13] Secondly, the traditional type of community was itself dying out, and giving way to less homogeneous, less autonomous, more impersonal social configurations.

The 'decline of community' theme is easily over-simplified, however, especially in a study of secularization. The very processes which undermined traditional rural communities, and by so doing damaged the parochial system of the Church, often abetted the growth of other religious movements, at least in the short run. John Wesley called the compact, nucleated village communities of 'lowland' England a 'Methodist desert', and wisely concentrated his efforts in London, in the colliery settlements at Kingswood, near Bristol, in the shipping, mining and manufacturing areas around Newcastle, where economic growth was in the process of disrupting traditional community solidarities, and in the rapidly-developing industrial heartlands of the West Riding, the West Midlands and the Black Country. Primitive Methodism, born in the first quarter of the nineteenth century, owed its early dramatic expansion to the receptiveness of people in the industrial villages and shanty settlements which, in the previous half-century, had mushroomed around factory towns and industrial cities. It also succeeded in agricultural villages, notably in Lincolnshire, where traditional community relationships had been disrupted, not by industrialization, but by agrarian capitalism, enclosure and an accompanying trend towards rural proletarianization. Religious deviance, in short, often capitalized upon the *disruption* of precisely those social configurations upon which the effectiveness of Anglicanism traditionally had depended.

Ominously, however, the great era of Methodist and Dissenting expansion was drawing to a close even before Victoria's reign began. Nonconformity would remain a strong element in Victorian culture, but not an expanding one. In the longer term the 'decline of community' would threaten it as much as it threatened the Church of England. For the early industrial age had been a period of transition, when old community patterns had been collapsing in the absence of new social structures to replace them. *Anomie* – a generalized feeling of insecurity, rootlessness, and social fragmentation reflecting a dearth of familiar institutions, associations and unifying social activities – was a feature of this, as of any other rapidly-changing society. Chapel communities were able, in such rudimentary circumstances, to meet associational, recreational and communal needs which in many cases would otherwise have gone unfulfilled. Alternative institutions, secular or religious, sometimes took years to develop, and in their absence the chapel became an obvious focus of social activity, providing its own microcosm of status, leadership and authority, its own networks of friendship, social co-operation and security.

Victorian Nonconformity's hostility to the worlds of the public house, the ballroom, the sporting club or indeed secular amusements generally, must be understood partly in this light. Certainly there were specifically 'religious' doubts about such things, but it is hard to avoid the idea that the fear of 'worldliness' was also partly a reaction, by the chapel community particularly, to the appearance of secular institutions offering the kinds of social, recreational and communal satisfactions over which it so recently had exercised a near monopoly in parts of the country. But whatever the force of such an interpretation, it is clear that the capacity of organized religion to benefit from a breakdown of traditional communal configurations in British society had been as temporary, as transitory, as the delay between the disruptive impact of modernizing economic changes and the emergence of a distinctively modern social order.

This modern social order may in fact be intrinsically *hostile* to religious habits and, perhaps, even to religious faith. Many scholars have argued that it is. 'We must face the inevitable', wrote a late nineteenth-century observer, looking forward to the twentieth century. 'The new civilization is certain to be urban; and the problem of the twentieth century will be the city.'[14] He went on to argue that the city epitomized the 'modern' tendency for a one-sided material affluence to predominate at the cost of moral and spiritual propensities. Subsequently, the idea of some sort of relationship between the nature of urban society and the emergence of materialistic, hedonistic forms of consciousness in the modern world has received considerable sociological attention. Spengler and Simmel, each a pioneer of urban sociology, investigated the nature of urban consciousness, and claimed to discover in 'metropolitan man' a distinctive mentality: rational, intellectual, and shaped by mechanical and artificial imperatives; blasé, cynical, and essentially withdrawn from personal contact with all but a small, inner core of friends and family. In a more academic analysis published during the First World War, R. E. Park, a founder of the 'Chicago School' of urban studies, defined the 'city mentality' in similar terms. So did Max Weber, and later David Riesman. And in perhaps the most arresting and pessimistic interpretation of all, Colin Bell and Harold Newby have included in their *Readings in the Sociology of Community* a thesis portraying life in the modern city as a process of de-humanization:

To believe . . . that human culture has reached a marvellous final culmination in the modern metropolis one must avert one's eyes from the grim details of the daily routine. And that is precisely what the metropolitan denizen schools himself to do: he lives, not in the real world, but in a shadow world projected around him at every moment by means of paper and celluloid and adroitly manipualted lights: a world in which he is insulated by glass, cellophane, pliofilm from the mortifications of living. In short, a world of professional illusionists and their credulous victims.[15]

It is of course possible to celebrate many of the things here criticised – to find creative possibilities in the new environment – yet still regard as inescapable the conclusion that the city itself, in its basic structures and essential social configurations, is a potent agent in the secularization of consciousness.

But quite apart from any impact it may have had on religious consciousness, urbanization has created an environment hostile, if not to associational religion *per se*, then at least to traditional modes of religious association and organization. In the first place, urbanization promotes and indeed demands high levels of spatial mobility. Following the pioneering work of French religious sociologists, and the testing of their hypotheses in America and elsewhere, it has become a commonplace of religious studies that migration from a rural community where religion is strong to an urban milieu where it lacks community identity is among the most powerful solvents of religious behaviour. But even where rural-to-urban migration is not involved, the exigencies of urban society promote spatial mobility within and between urban environments. Education, marriage, changes in employment or promotion to a higher level of employment, enhanced wealth and status, retirement or bereavement – these and other experiences are for the urban dweller very often occasions for changes of residence and locality. And a 'sense of place' – of loyalty to geographically definable institutions like a parish church or a village chapel – is weakened progressively by such changes.

This does not mean, as is sometimes suggested, that the urban population is rootless and anomic. Rather it means that the social identity of the urbanite, like the associational and communal relationships and institutional involvements which define his social status and social roles, are no longer primarily territorial. There has been no permanent 'decline of community' *per se*. What the city has done is differentiate community functions in the context of a new cultural pluralism. The single, cohesive, totalitarian community of traditional village society has given way to a pluralistic situation in which a single individual is involved, segmentally, in a number of partial communities. A sense of community based on geographical location rarely ceases to exist, but in an urban environment it must compete for the loyalty of its members with their prior commitments to other types of community sense.

Organized religion, everywhere in the British Isles, has failed to cope with the decline of the territorial community and the emergence of pluralistic, partial communities. The idea of territoriality remains central to Christian planning, both pastoral and evangelistic, and church leaders still tend to think of work among newer, functional communities, as 'special ministries'. Service, industrial and prison chaplaincies, ministries to the young and the aged, to holiday-camp communities, to students, to ethnic minorities and other similar 'partial communities', have been much-discussed and often instigated. But they remain peripheral in relation to overall effort and expenditure in all the major denominations, and arguments as to whether such ministries can function as authentic 'churches', with full sacramental prerogatives, reflect the deep-seated assumption that a 'real' church must have some territorial identity.

The Church of England, although more progressive than its rivals in adapting to the new situation, nevertheless illustrates the enormous inertial resistance to change characteristic of the traditional organizing principle based on the territorial parish. By 1970 about 2,000 Anglican clergy, almost one-seventh of the total engaged in active Christian ministries, exercised non-parochial, 'special' functions, and their number included priests working in radio and television and clerical assistants attached to the Church's Central Boards of administration. Their role within the Church remained essentially marginal. Often they faced the jealousy of the ordinary parish priests struggling to find a satisfying role within increasingly amorphous parochial 'communities', for they seemed to the latter to have 'opted out of the system'. Noting this, a Working Party set up by the Church to look into 'specialized ministries' reported that it remained a fact of life in modern Anglicanism that 'the parochial ministry always has priority on finance'.[16]

In such circumstances institutional secularization is inevitable in the modern social environment. An American scholar has spoken of a 'cognitive lag' between church organization and changing patterns of community. Distinguishing between modern, partial communities defined by function – communities of work, communities of leisure, communities of learning, etc – and traditional communities of place, or 'turf', he has remarked that the contemporary churches are in difficulties because 'virtually all their language, structures, and even values are shaped by turf-orientation'. As the 'cognitive lag' is overcome, he has concluded, we can expect to see modern religious organizations of a radically new, newly effective kind.[17]

In Britain, however, equally perceptive diagnosis has been followed by much less optimistic prognosis. After a masterly analysis of emerging social configurations in industrial south-west Wales, a commission set up by the Blaendulais Ecumenical Centre reported in 1969 that 'A mobile living society confronts a comparatively immobile Church . . .'. But the problem went well beyond mere 'cognitive lag'. The commission warned that 'churches (like many other institutions) tend to act only *in extremis*'.[18] At present, in all British Churches, structural adaptation remains both slow and superficial, and the out-moded character of Christianity's age-old organizing principle of territoriality serves only to compound the cultural problems arising from the rational and artificial nature of modern urban society.

## CLASS, POLITICS AND SECULARIZATION

Traditional communities were not without social divisions based on wealth and status, but they were not 'class' societies in the modern sense. A class is an entity at once social and cultural. It is a stratified social division based on such major socio-economic characteristics as common economic circumstances and rewards, affinities of social status, living conditions and political power, and major objective differences distinguishing it from other socio-economic strata. Culturally, it involves shared values, norms and assumptions about social reality, consciousness of horizontal identities and vertical antagonisms within the society, and a sense of group solidarity across the whole 'class' stratum. In a 'class' society, in short, the primary social and cultural solidarities are horizontal, while the primary tensions, conflicts and antagonisms are vertical.

Pre-industrial Britain was not such a society. Certainly it was stratified, both in objective socio-economic terms and in the perceptions of its members. But it was a highly localized society. A locality was the primary focus of social identity and communal loyalty for the bulk of the population. The aristocracy and gentry who thought and acted nationally (or at least regionally), as well as locally, were a tiny minority of the nation, In a sense they – and they alone – formed a 'class'. For other Britons the vertical social divisions dictated by locality formed communal solidarities capable of transcending the undeniable horizontal stratifications of wealth, power and status. Animosities between social strata in such societies did exist, and produced what E.P. Thompson has called 'pre-figurations of nineteenth century class attitudes and organization'.[19] Yet the fact remains that in pre-industrial society the central organizing and cultural realities reflected a consciousness of *vertical* solidarities. The dominant vertical relationships involved 'dependencies' based on the practice of deference, among the common people, and paternalism among their social superiors. Community cohesion arising from this 'dependency system' was what had given the social and political structure of pre-industrial society, as well as its ecclesiastical organization, a distinctive character.

Because the Anglican and Presbyterian Establishments were implicated deeply in the politics of deference and dependency – historically, organizationally, and through the social backgrounds, values and alliances of their clergy – their influence and their relevance suffered as class structure and class consciousness gradually assumed predominance in Britain. Religious statistics indicate that of the major regions of the British Isles, only Northern Ireland has experienced more or less general increases in religious participation in recent years, and it is significant that Ulster stands out as the only part of the United Kingdom in which vertical social configurations (reinforced and symbolized by traditional religious allegiances), have remained more important than class as determinants of the basic social structure. In contrast, in England and Wales the advent of class politics had begun, even before the First World War, to destroy the Victorian alignment of party-political and Church-chapel rivalry which had provided the major Protestant bodies with guaranteed social prominence.

Almost the only matter upon which Gladstonian Liberals and Disraelian Conservatives had agreed was the undesirability of independent working-class political power. Disraeli had used Tory paternalism and imperial patriotism to shape a late-Victorian conservativism which addressed its appeal across emerging class lines; Gladstone had exploited a succession of 'great issues' to maintain the Liberal Party as a classless coalition of progressive elements in the society. This 'defeat of class', George Watson has observed, 'is the most important of all the facts to record' in a history of Victorian political life.[20] As far as the relationship between religion and politics is concerned there can be no doubt about the truth of the observation, for religious leaders, issues and institutions were kept firmly at the centre of public life by such matters as Irish Disestablishment (which dominated the election of 1868), state involvement in education (which was a major political issue between 1870 and the 1874 election, as it would be again after the 1902 Education Act), and to a somewhat lesser extent by the political debates prompted by the Eastern Question, Irish Home Rule and the Parnell affair. Recognizing the importance of this religion–politics alignment in the political battles of 1868–69, Gladstone had written:

Our three *corps d'armée*, I may almost say, have been Scotch Presbyterians, English and Welsh nonconformists, and Irish Roman Catholics. . . . The England clergy as a body have done their worst against us and have hit us hard. . . .[21]

It had been the kind of confrontation upon which Gladstonian Liberalism had thrived.

But with the Third Reform Act political power in Britain began to pass to a social majority for whom such issues were largely irrelevant. As Joseph Chamberlain's *Radical Programme* put it in 1884: 'New conceptions of public duty, new developments of social enterprise, new estimates of the natural obligations of the members of the community to one another, have come into view and demand consideration'.[22] The Liberal Party rejected the *Radical Programme*, lost the allegiance of

Chamberlain, and clung to Gladstone during the crisis of 1886 precipitated by Irish Home Rule. In so doing it lost an opportunity – a final opportunity, perhaps – to catch the tide of class politics upon which, within a generation, a Labour Party yet unborn would sweep to the centre of national politics. The stubbornness of Gladstonian Liberalism gave Church-chapel rivalry a last, spectacular moment of glory during the great education crisis of 1902-06. But if the old, anti-class tactics generated an electoral landslide in 1906, the fact remained that within two decades of 1906 the Liberal Party was doomed.

Historians and political scientists continue to argue about the precise nature of the Party's malady, about the point in time when pathological tendencies became terminal, and about the relative importance, in the decline process, of party-political blunders as distinct from immutable social changes. But the facts are patent. By the early 1920s the Labour Party had become the major anti-Conservative force in a system of Westminster politics in which both sides operated essentially on the assumption that Britain had become a class society.

The advent of class as the basis of British politics was a consequence of its predominant role in twentieth-century British society, and at both the political and the social level the change went hand in hand with the advance of secularization. The rise of class exercised this counter-religious influence for two reasons. The first reflected the historical context in which class consciousness and class conflict had taken shape; the second reflected the significance for the society as a whole of the early and almost complete dechristianization of the British working classes. Both points require some elaboration.

Historically, British working-class consciousness evolved partly as a process of rejection, by the once-deferential 'lower orders', of the vertical relationships of dependency in which the Established Church had been deeply implicated. Rejecting the squire usually meant rejecting the parson as well, especially because so many parsons of the late eighteenth and early nineteenth centuries combined the roles of landowner and magistrate with their pastoral duties. Thus both the idea and the reality of the State Church gave the 'birth of class' an essentially counter-religious significance. Early working-class leaders, however much they professed religious belief and used Biblical rhetoric, attacked 'priestcraft' as a reactionary political symbol and the Established Church as a manifestation of prescriptive authority and entrenched privilege. Their followers generally lost their Anglicanism, such as it was, along with their deference.

Relating religion and class obviously becomes more complicated in the case of Nonconformity. Perkin, for example, has called religious deviance the 'midwife' of class, and gone as far as to suggest that the growth of Nonconformist communities is the best available index of 'emancipation from the system of dependency'.[23] The evidence supports such a view. Methodism, especially in its non-Wesleyan varieties, and the New Dissent of the early industrial age did, in certain contexts, operate as semi-legitimate forms of social protest against a reactionary Establishment. Primitive Methodism dominated working-class activities on the Durham coalfields during the tense confrontations of the 1840s, and as late as the 1870s some rural chapel communities fulfilled similar functions at a time when the formation of the Agricultural Labourers' Union was signalling the emergence of rural working-class consciousness.

The role of midwife is transitory, however. Whatever it contributed to the birth of class, Nonconformity quickly lost touch with the maturing working-class culture of the Victorian era. As early as the Census of Religion of 1851 the social geography of the movement showed a heavy bias towards middle-class areas, and as the Victorian years lengthened Nonconformist social alignments and policies often provoked a justifiable proletarian suspicion that what was being mediated was (in modern political parlance), the hegemony of one class over another. Temperance societies, Sunday-schools, Home Missionary activities, and indeed most chapel-sponsored enterprises in working-class districts could be seen in this light. The fact, rightly emphasised by one recent historian, that Sunday-schools 'grew out of the working class', does not, as he implies, disqualify them from the role of leading a 'bourgeois assault on working-class culture'.[24] It may simply reflect the slow and piecemeal development of class consciousness in Britain. The fact is that, whether deservedly or not, Christianity *generally* – not just the Established Anglican version of it – seemed to many a working man, in the words of John Trevor, founder of the ephemeral Labour Church, to 'cheerfully accept, and in many cases . . . stubbornly defend, the things against which it is his mission to fight'.[25]

If imputations of possible class prejudice in British religious culture remain somewhat tendentious, there can be no question about working-class *estrangement* on matters of religion. From occupying, however precariously, an integral role in a vertical system of pre-industrial social relationships, religion has become, in a class society, an almost exclusively middle and upper-class activity, and in its respectable milieu it has retained almost nothing of the integrative role once exercised in the maintenance of vertical solidarities. This estrangement may have begun in pre-industrial society, as Thompson, among others, has suggested,[26] but it did so in response to early symptoms of modernization. For it is clear that the decisive factors have been urbanization and industrialization. 'It is not that the Church of England has lost the great towns,' an Anglican Bishop observed in 1896, 'it has never had them . . .'.[27]

' "We don't want your gospel, we want a new social order!" say the average men.' Thus the *Methodist Times* summarized working-class attitudes in the Rhondda Valley after the First World War.[28] It was a sombre acknowledgment of a recent change. For Welsh Nonconformity, like the stern calvinism of the Scottish Free Churches, was exceptional in the British religious situation in that it did retain significant appeal for working-class people into the early years of the twentieth century. Its persistence in working-class contexts does not, however, negate the notion of a basic incompatibility between traditional religiosity and the social values of the modern proletarian culture. It merely reflects the relatively slower development, in Wales and elsewhere, of the kinds of social attitudes, structures and institutions which matured first among the English working classes. At its zenith in the late Victorian period, for example, Welsh Nonconformity 'never lost the attitude of a "gathered church" to its contemporary society'. As E. T. Davies has pointed out in an impressive study, its consistent objective was 'to call people out of the "world" into the "church" '. The result, he has recognized, was a Nonconformist religiosity serving individuals while ignoring working-class culture; and 'while it dominated the early history of the industrial society', the movement 'never became responsible for that society as a whole.' Its appeal was to 'the spiritual individualism of people ready to accept that "the world was well lost" '.[29]

By the end of the First World War working-class culture was turning away from such assumptions. In the previous decade or so Liberal Party allegiances based on the chapel community had given way to Labour politics based on the Trade Unions and the new working-men's clubs; and simultaneously, other-worldly individualism had given way so emphatically to melioristic socialism that South Wales was becoming, along with Clydeside and the old Methodist strongholds of north-eastern England, one of the most socialist areas in the British Isles. A major challenge, Welsh Christians have recognized, is for the chapel to regain *significance 'vis-à-vis* other social institutions where *power* is centred.' In part, the solution may be, as the Blaendulais Survey has concluded, 'rather like a difficult engineering job which involves radical changes in the structure of a building'.[30] Yet the question begged by the class orientation of modern Welsh culture is whether social engineering, however radical, can turn back the tide of secularization.

It is a vital question partly because the existence of a virtually unchurched working class has profound implications for the impact of secularization on *all* classes in modern British society. For several reasons, a religion grounded in proletarian culture would have provided the strongest bulwark against secularization. The cultural consequences of affluence and material security *may* have had less impact on such Christians. The social consequences of spatial mobility and the 'decline of community' would certainly have affected them least. Hugh McLeod, in an analysis distinguishing between neighbourhood, district, regional and 'national and international' conceptions of community, has remarked that it was precisely the working classes who were, and are, most likely to identify strongly with a locality or neighbourhood. Other social groups tend to be more mobile, and to resort to a greater spread and variety of social relationships and institutional foci. In short, of all social classes in an industrial society, the working class retains the closest structural affinity to the unitary type of community based on territoriality. The Churches are thus estranged most completely, in a cultural sense, from the very groups whose social habits they are best suited to serve; and they depend, almost exclusively, upon the allegiance of other sections of the society – the middle classes – for whom the traditional 'community of residence', and traditional pattern of religious organization, are least suited.

Moreover, the dechristianized working classes have become, in a real sense, the arbiters of the critical cultural forces which still succeed in transcending class barriers. There is no single 'popular culture' in modern Britain, but various cultural forces have emerged to serve and shape the interests of all classes. The media, especially television, provide obvious examples. So do major sporting traditions. And most of all, perhaps, so do certain of the values, expectations and assumptions implicit in the language and objectives of modern consumer advertising. To the extent that advertising operates as a general cultural influence, culture generally comes to reflect market forces, purchasing power, consumer-oriented consciousness. Until the present century these very forces consigned working-class culture to a marginal role in national life; but in the twentieth century, as Richard Hoggart observed twenty years ago, they now make the working classes, in aggregate, the major arbiters of popular consciousness. Thus in the modern society it is not only the most numerous, but also in a sense the most truly 'hegemonic' class which is least influenced by Christian thought and Christian institutions.

## RECREATION, LEISURE AND SECULARIZATION

Chapter Three has argued that the vastly increased material wealth and productive capacity of the industrial society encouraged the growth of a modern hedonistic culture. The change reflected, among other things, a clear rationalization of the differences between work and leisure, and an institutionalization of new forms of recreation. But while these latter changes in the social habits and institutions of the society did, in fact, reinforce the secularizing impact of hedonistic consciousness, it requires a careful argument to show why they had this significance. For increased leisure need not necessarily have been a source of secularization. Indeed, the initial Christianization of European culture had involved the sacralization, by the Church, of many of the rituals and recreational practices of pagan life, including the use of bells, candles, incense, singing and dancing. Miracle and morality plays, festivals prescribed by the Church Calendar, wakes, fairs, nuptial and other familial celebrations, and indeed the recurrent occasions of communal conviviality provided by regular religious services all guaranteed the pre-industrial Church a basic role in community life.

What made modern developments in recreational culture so damaging to traditional religious institutions was their effect in transforming the role of the Churches from a 'basic' to a 'serving' one. This is a useful sociological distinction. A 'basic' insitution is one which determines, or helps to determine, 'the nature of the community in which it is situated', whereas a 'serving' institution is one which, to survive, must search for ways to serve its clientele. People cannot, in short, ignore the basic institutions of their society without endangering the social order, but a social order will remain intact without its serving institutions. Where the latter are concerned involvement is optional, and for this reason one such institution ultimately is in competition with all others for social patronage.[31]

For the Christian Church the transition from basic to serving institution had started with the Renaissance. As Chapter Two has argued, secular tendencies in politics, education and the arts had at that time begun to erode the medieval civilization in which Catholicism had been basic. And the tendencies had continued despite mounting ecclesiastical opposition. By the end of the sixteenth century, music, dance and theatre had begun to spawn discrete professions in England, and were attracting secular patronage. Even earlier Sunday football and tennis had become so popular that Richard II had felt obliged to ban them – albeit in the secular hope of encouraging more archery practice! Religious opposition, on the other hand, had represented an early counter-attack on secularization. As varieties of sport, recreation and entertainment had grown apart from the life of the Church and the role of the clergy, the latter, seeking to maintain their traditional authority, had embarked on a prolonged campaign of eradiction or curtailment.

For almost three centuries after the Reformation it had been a campaign in which defeats had not been decisive and victory had always seemed possible. If by the eve of the Industrial Revolution Anglicans had, in Thompson's words, 'lost command over the "leisure" of the poor, their feasts and festivals, and, with this, over a large area of plebeian culture',[32] the loss had not yet assumed an appearance of permanence. A counter-attack had begun in the form of Methodism, New Dissent and Evangelical Anglicanism, and as Thompson himself was forced to concede in his unhappy recognition of the impact of Methodism on the embryonic English working class of the early nineteenth century, the counter-attack had met with considerable success. It had had much to do, for example, with the emergence of a Victorian bourgeois culture paying lip service, at least, to puritanical standards of public behaviour, including strict Sabbatarianism. Through the so-called 'Nonconformist Conscience', the Victorian Churches had managed to exert an informal, but powerful, censorial control over patterns of public recreation and entertainment.

In the twentieth century, however, British Christianity has paid dearly for its historic assertion of hegemony over recreational culture. It had been an assertion which a 'basic' institution might have made with impunity – and would not really have had to make at all; but for religious organizations slowly being relegated to the status of 'serving' institutions it had been a precarious enterprise. In a secularizing society, particularly one as divided as Victorian Britain, the success of the Churches in imposing religious sanctions on the recreations and pastimes of the middle classes had two significant disadvantages. First, by associating religiosity with the tastes, habits and outlook of bourgeois respectability, it exacerbated the estrangement between Christianity and working-class culture. Secondly, it produced a situation in which the Churches found themselves, almost unavoidably, in competition with 'modern' trends in recreational culture.

If the early Methodists had capitalized on the dearth of recreational facilities in the primitive phase of industrialization, and then faced the challenge of having to retain members as the maturing industrial society evolved secular alternatives to the recreational satisfactions of the chapel community, all the major Churches were eventually forced into the same kind of position as a result of their negative attitudes to secular pleasures and pastimes. By forcing potential clients to choose between themselves and the 'new paganism' of worldly recreations they courted rejection. Negativism supported no longer by the social dominance of a basic institution would lead towards narrow sectarianism. So the temptation to turn religion into a competing entertainment often assumed irresistible proportions, and the late-Victorian Churches increasingly shouldered the responsibility 'of supplying healthy entertainments for the masses and various forms of sociability for the middle-classes.' But it was a strategy which, however obvious, was doomed to failure by the emerging social realities of the modern industrial world. In a thoughtful discussion of *Institutional Religion*, published as part of the Church of England's 'Affirmations' series in 1930, J. C. Hardwick wrote:

> This policy is clearly doomed to failure under present conditions, though it succeeded well enough during the closing decades of the nineteenth century, before the rise of cinemas, wireless, the cheap motor-car, and a whole galaxy of inexpensive amusements. . . . The distracted and disillusioned incumbent of an industrial (or even a rural) parish to-day knows too well that he can never hope to rival the cinema, the dance hall, the dirt-track, the working men's club, the public billiard hall, the domestic loud-speaker, the well-cushioned charabanc, or the cheap motor-bicycle. All he can hope to do, ill equipped as he is, is to offer an inferior article with a little edification thrown in to compensate the consumer, but this does not go down in the modern world, and only exposes those who hope so to humiliations. This attempt to draw a non-religious public to church by lures of this kind no longer works. Our bait is inferior, or judged to be so by those who are asked to take it, the only people whose taste need be considered.[33]

As serving institutions in a secular society the Churches would have been adversely affected by modern developments in recreational culture whatever their strategies, but the ambivalent position inherited from the nineteenth century – of seeking simultaneously both to censor secular entertainments and to compete with them – left modern religious institutions particularly vulnerable to challenges arising from the secularization of leisure. Among these challenges two developments have been especially significant.

## The secularization of Sunday

Sabbatarianism had been made into a pillar of Victorian Christianity in Britain. The Lord's Day Observance Act of 1780, the closing of public houses on Sundays (from 1854), and, from 1855, the banning of Sunday newspapers, together with the closure on Sundays of barber shops and tobacconists, were simply legislative equivalents of the social mores –

informal but even more restrictive – which sought to make Sunday a time for churchgoing, seriousness, sombre dress, and the avoidance of normal work and pleasure. The setting aside of a particular day for religious practice is not, according to the apostle Paul, an essential of correct Christian behaviour, but it became so in the basic symbolism and institutional expression of Victorian Christianity. And for this reason, its decline both signified and hastened an erosion of religious commitment in the society.

Evidence of the decline of the Victorian 'Sabbath' was causing concern before the nineteenth century closed. Even among the middle classes, clergy reported as early as the 1890s, Sunday seemed to be devolving into no more than 'a day of physical rest' – or worse, into an occasion for sport or recreation.[34] Moreover, the trend appears to have been well-established by the time clerical anxiety became widespread. Since the middle of the nineteenth century rising incomes, shorter working hours and cheap public transport had mounted a growing threat to Sabbatarian principles, and the working-class National Sunday League, founded in 1875, had begun to voice the opposition of the unchurched sections of the community to legal strictures against the secularization of Sunday. Its object was to make Sunday a time when rest and recreation would be facilitated by the opening of public houses, museums, art galleries, theatres and (later) cinemas, and by the availability of adequate public transport.

As the non-churchgoers have won their battle in the modern world, the secularized Sunday has become a temptation which the churchgoing classes evidently have found it difficult to resist. As early as 1900, even without legislation, half-day holidays on Saturdays had become widespread, and as the idea of paid holidays and reduced working hours received public acceptance and legislative endorsement (culminating in the Holidays with Pay Act of 1938), the traditional 'Sabbath' inevitably was subsumed by the modern, secular concept of the 'week-end'. If it survived at all, churchgoing tended both to become less frequent – the three-times-a-day churchgoer, common in 1850, would today be found only in small, intense sectarian movements; the once-a-fortnight churchgoer, the monthly or quarterly attendant, is now cited by optimistic Christian sociologists as evidence against secularization! On a fairly generous interpretation of available data, David Martin estimated in 1967 that 15 per cent of the English population attended some religious service on an average Sunday, that 20 per cent attended over a typical two-Sunday period, and that 25 per cent went to church at least once in an average month. On the other hand, 1 person in 5 entered a church only for life's rites of passage, and

35 per cent of the population never attended at all.[35] Between 1968 and 1974, moreover, rates of Anglican attendance fell by 12 per cent and Catholic attendance at Sunday Mass fell by more than 16 per cent.[36] Churchgoing, in short, had become a minority habit in the modern British 'world', and J. A. R. Pimlott's 'Farewell to the British Sunday?', published in *New Society* a few years earlier, might well have dispensed with its question-mark.[37]

## Mobility and privatization

A Harris Poll commissioned by the *Daily Express* in April 1970 asked a sample of people from all parts of Britain why church attendance has declined in the modern world. By far the most popular answer – given more than twice as often as any other – was that there are simply 'Too many distractions' – television, bingo, and motor cars, the respondents suggested, were major counter-religious attractions. Other common answers which possibly implied the same kind of diagnosis included the idea that, 'People do not have the spare time nowadays', and the observation that 'People are lazy, can't be bothered'.[38]

It is interesting to note that of the three hostile influences actually specified, television, bingo and the motor car, only one can be regarded as the same kind of social activity as churchgoing. Bingo, like theatre-going or spectator sport, is an associational activity involving a type of spatial congregation not unlike the social act of church attendance. The television set and the motor car, on the other hand, symbolize two distinctly modern social patterns which have undermined churchgoing habits. They do not establish competing activities of a similar associational kind, they instead threaten organized religion by disrupting traditional associational patterns altogether. These modern tendencies may be summarized by the words *mobility* and *privatization*.

A combination of increased leisure and cheap rail transport had offered a mobility previously undreamed of to the great bulk of the British population of the late nineteenth and early twentieth centuries. Within a generation or so its inevitable impact on social habits had become the subject of social inquiry. Seebohm Rowntree stressed 'the tremendous importance of railway and bus excursions' when he surveyed social behaviour in York in the late 1930s, and pointed out that the 'week-end habit' of recreational travel had been well-established among all classes.[39] This development must have affected Sunday church attendances, but it has been the motor car which has had the greatest impact. Any possibility that the traditional community of residence, on which religious organization is still based, would remain an important community of recreation (outside the individual family), has evaporated as motor vehicle registrations have risen.

As late as 1974 only 56 per cent of British households possessed at least one motor vehicle, although many others had weekend access to a vehicle belonging to an employer. But levels of ownership among middle and upper income groups – precisely the most church-orientated classes – was well above the national average. Pimlott noted in 1964 that on Whit Sunday British roads had been congested by a record nine million cars! And the motor car meant not just greater mobility; it meant mobility of a new, private, personal kind. It emancipated Sunday activities from the tyranny of the clock and freed family recreation from the public involvements of bus-stop and railway station. Thus while its contribution to family mobility further reduced the importance of residence as a determinant of social behaviour, its contribution to family autonomy in leisure and recreation reinforced the modern trend towards the privatization of social life.[40]

Privatization is a luxury of the affluent society. Functions and services once available only in public situations, and only in close co-operation with a wider community, become available in a modern society either in the privacy of a family home or through minimal, impersonal contact with service organizations. Leisure and recreation provide the most obvious examples of the change, notably in the media of radio and television. The first BBC programme was broadcast in November 1922, and within three years 1,140,000 licences were issued. Radio audiences peaked in the 1940s, before the impact of television, but even in 1964 20 million Britons spent 90 minutes at midday on Sundays listening to 'Family Favourites'. It is true that this privatization of leisure was checked in the 1930s and 1940s by the cinema boom, which at its zenith in 1946 averaged attendances of 30 million per week, but not even the cinema could withstand the impact of television. BBC television began officially in 1936, when only 300 receivers were in private hands, but its real growth was postponed until after the Second World War. Licence numbers rose from 11,000 in 1938 to 6.4 million in 1957. By 1964 12.8 million homes had licences, and by 1976 the number was 18 million.[41]

Television, especially, tends to keep the modern family in the home, at least when the family car is not providing an alternative form of private recreation. It undermines public patterns of leisure as well as public acts of religious worship. Indeed, as early as 1961 more than half of the total adult population of Britain spent Sunday evening either listening to the radio or watching television.[42] By 1976 the average weekly hours spent watching television amounted to between 15 and 20 per cent of the total waking hours of the population aged five years and over.[43] These are arresting figures, providing powerful evidence of the capacity of the modern media to dictate patterns of social behaviour. They also mirror perhaps the most intractable of all the social manifestations of secularization.

Given that traditional patterns of religious practice have failed to withstand, among other things, this trend towards privatization, it is easy to pronounce that the Churches should be trying harder to adapt their religious culture to the novel social reality. The need for adaptation is obvious and urgent, but it is by no means certain that effective adaptation is even possible. Arguably, the most alarming of all religious statistics as far as the Churches are concerned is the fact that, despite the strength of the viewing habit, 16 per cent of the British television audience actually 'switch off' when a religious programme appears, and another 24 per cent 'leave the set on but don't really listen'.[44]

# NOTES

1. Gilbert, A. D. (1976), pp. 27–9, 94–121. Cf. Gay, J. D. (1971), Maps 8–9, 27, 35, 43–4, pp. 271–310.
2. Gilbert, A. D. (1976), pp. 27–9, 125–8.
3. Ward, W. R. (1965).
4. Clark, G. K. (1965), p. 162.
5. Gilbert, A. D. (1976), pp. 162–74; Jones, I. G. (1961); Koss, S. (1975); Mackintosh, W. H. (1972); Morgan, K. O. (1970); Vincent, J. (1966); and Yeo, S. (1976).
6. Morgan, K. O. (1970), p. 218.
7. Currie, R., Gilbert, A. D. and Horsley, L. H. (1977).
8. Ibid., pp. 29–30.
9. Ibid., pp. 72–4, 128–89.
10. Ibid., pp. 64–74, 79–90.
11. Gilbert, A. D. (1976), pp. 59–68, 145–49; Inglis, K. S. (1963), *passim.*
12. *Quarterly Review*, XXIII (1820), p. 564.
13. Yates, R. (1815), p. 159.
14. Josiah Strong, quoted by Weber, M. (1958), p. 18.
15. Bell, C. and Newby, H. (1974), pp. 547–8.
16. *Specialised Ministries* (1971), p. 35.
17. Ramsden, W. E. (1971), pp. 171–2.
18. Jones, V. (1969), p. 91.
19. Thompson, E. P. (1974), p. 398.
20. Watson, G. (1973), p. 188.
21. Feuchtwanger, E. J. (1975), p. 145.

22. Thompson, J. A. (1969), p. 26.
23. Perkin, H. (1969), p. 197.
24. Lacqueur, T. W. (1976), p. 189.
25. Quoted by Inglis, K. S. (1963), p. 219.
26. Thompson, E. P. (1974), *passim.*
27. Quoted by Inglis, K. S. (1963), p. 3.
28. *Methodist Times*, 4 May 1922.
29. Davies, E. T. (1965), pp. 94–6. Cf. Brennan, T., Cooney, E. W. and Pollins, M. (1954).
30. Jones, V. (1969), p. 116.
31. For an elaboration of this distinction, see Hughes, E. C. (1936), pp. 180–9.
32. Thompson, E. P. (1974), p. 402.
33. Hardwick, J. C. (1930), p. 17.
34. McLeod, H. (1974), p. 235.
35. Martin, D. (1967), p. 43.
36. Thompson, E. J. (1976), p. 178.
37. *New Society*, 22 October 1964.
38. The Harris Poll, 'The Religious Beliefs of the British People' (Report on a Survey Carried out from 13–19 April, 1970), p. 7.
39. Quoted by Johnson, W., Whyman, J. and Wykes, G. (1967), pp. 191–2.
40. Thompson, E. J. (1976), pp. 133, 214.
41. Johnson, W., Whyman, J. and Wykes, G. (1967), p. 197; Thompson, E. J. (1976), p. 183.
42. Halsey, A. H. (1972), p. 554.
43. A calculation based on data in Table 10.20 in Thompson, E. S. (1976), p. 83.
44. Independent Television Authority (1970), p. 39.

# PART THREE   61565
# *Churches in a post-Christian world*

'What reverence is rightly paid
To a Divinity so odd
He lets the Adam whom He made
Perform the Acts of God?

(W. H. Auden, 'Friday's Child', from *Homage to Clio*)

# The Christian dilemma in a post-Christian world

How have the Churches reacted to a world grown more secular? The question can be answered at two levels. Some ecclesiastical responses have been conscious and deliberate. Organizational strategies, evangelistic methods, pastoral techniques, and even the language, emphases and principles of Christian theology have been adjusted to accommodate, or to resist, the exigencies of the modern environment. But important changes have also occurred as Christians and Christian organizations have adjusted more or less unconsciously to their secular surroundings, and the conscious and deliberate responses to secularization have sometimes been over-shadowed by the promptings of latent motives and purposes. But whether latent or manifest, responses of the modern 'Church' to the secular 'world' can be classified in terms of a distinction between *accommodation* and *resistance*.

Accommodation is an essentially 'denominational' response. In terms of the important sociological distinction between 'Church' and 'denomination', the crucial difference is that whereas the Church claims unique legitimacy, monopolistic control over the religiosity of its constituent population, and exclusive ecclesiastical authority, the denomination accepts the legitimacy of other forms of Christianity operates on the assumption of religious pluralism within a single society, and makes no claim to exclusive authority. In these terms, the mainstream of modern British Christianity must be regarded as essentially denominational. Anglicanism no longer asserts exclusive legitimacy. Its residual churchly advantages as the 'State Church' notwithstanding, it operates for all practical purposes simply as the largest of a plurality of legitimate institutional options. Like any other denomination it claims particular advantages for its own forms of policy and religious culture, but the claim is accompanied by recognition of the legitimacy and value of other traditions.

The position of the Catholic Church in Britain, examined in the context of this sociological distinction, is admittedly ambiguous. As part of an international 'Church' still asserting, if not always practising, exclusive legitimacy within Christianity, British Catholicism sometimes adopts a churchly stance. But as a minority movement within British religion it often appears to accept the logic of genuine religious pluralism. There have been many echoes, for example, of the call in the 1940s by Michael de la Bedoyere, editor of the *Catholic Herald*, for Catholics, Anglicans and Nonconformists to 'co-operate sincerely and with generous Christian minds' in order to defend 'the dogma and moral teaching of Christianity in the face of a semi-pagan world'.[1]

This is an interesting statement partly because it reflects a third element in modern Catholic religious culture – an element also present, in varying proportions, in all the essentially denominational traditions. It is the idea of a Christianity embattled in a hostile cultural environment, of irrepressible conflict between the 'churches' and the 'world'. This is not a typically denominational position. It is an incongruity reflecting the impact of secularization. The denominational tendency is to endorse the dominant values, norms and assumptions of the wider culture, and to accept the appropriateness of a limited, segmental influence for Christian principles within it. Indeed, a situation of denominational pluralism usually reflects a degree of differentiation arising from the *identification* of particular denominations with distinct class, regional or ethnic divisions within a society.

Being involved so directly in secular social realities predisposes denominationalism, consciously and unconsciously, towards accommodatory responses to secularization. As a voluntary, segmental form of religiosity, the denominational culture seeks to attract adherents without demanding that they reject other associations, or deviate from accepted social norms. It seeks acceptance and significance by being a kind of conscience for the wider society, or for certain elements of it; but as this very role implies, it avoids fundamental opposition to the conventional morals, values and properties of the age. It is, in the caustic words of H. Richard Niebuhr's classic study, 'a Christianity which surrenders its leadership to the social forces of national and economic life. . . '.[2] Its very nature, Niebuhr insisted, involves 'compromise . . . between Christianity and the world'.[3]

Bedoyere's vision of the need for Christian action *against* a world already semi-pagan, and still under-going secularization, cannot therefore be regarded as a mainstream response in a denominational situation. Indeed, it is a frankly anti-denominational vision. Its premise is that if the 'Church' can no longer dictate faith and morals to the wider culture – if its traditional churchly role becomes untenable in a secular age – then it is not a denominational response which is appropriate, but a 'sectarian' one. For if the denominational response involves accommodation, the hallmark of the sect is resistance. The sect, like the genuine 'church-type' of religiosity and unlike the denomination, claims exclusive legitimacy, for its religious-cultural position if not always for its particular collectivity. Its orientation to the wider society is sub-cultural, and sometimes expressly counter-cultural; and the consequence of its rejection of worldly values, assumptions and norms is, on the one hand, that it can expect only minority support, and, on the other, that it can command intense loyalty from those willing to make an initial sectarian commitment.

Chapters Five and Six seek to explore the ways in which the modern British Churches have met the critical choice between accommodation and resistance with which secularization has confronted them. It is a dilemma becoming ever more agonizing. In the case of the denomination, the price of accommodation was relatively low so long as the wider culture retained much of the legacy of its historic Christianization. But in a post-Christian age, Chapter Five argues, to continue choosing accommodatory options may be to risk a vital paganization of Christianity. And for the sect, so long as there was a flourishing denominational tradition resistance could be expressed largely within a Christian cultural milieu. In the future, however, if secularization proceeds unchecked, a sectarian 'remnant' seems likely to lose this 'lukewarm' environment, this vague Christian *a priori*, and to find itself exposed completely to the cold indifference of a post-Christian world. Yet such is the crisis of contemporary British Christianity, Chapter Six argues, that the sectarian option of resistance to secularization may offer the only realistic strategy for the future.

## NOTES

1. De la Bedoyere, M. (n.d.), p. 181.
2. Neibuhr, H. Richard (1957), p. 275.
3. Ibid., p. 6.

# CHAPTER FIVE

# The secularization of the Church

The accommodation of the 'Church' to a 'world' grown more secular – the secularization of modes of thought and patterns of behaviour *within* the religious culture itself – has been, without doubt, the dominant trend in modern British religious history. It is illuminating to compare the results of this process with the related, yet far from identical, effects of secularization on American religion. In American society, Peter Berger has written,

the churches operate with secular values while the secular institutions are permeated with religious terminology. In both cases, the terminology is derived from the often referred to Judaeo-Christian tradition, though it has been radically voided of the religious contents it possessed in this tradition. The terminology now applies to a vague religiosity which Will Herberg has called the 'common faith' and Martin Marty has described as 'religion-in-general'. Since this religiosity is held both within and without the religious institution proper, an objective observer is hard put to tell the difference (at least in terms of values affirmed) between the church members and those who maintain an 'unchurched' status. Usually the most that can be said is that the church members hold the same values as everybody else, but with more emphatic solemnity. Thus, church membership in no way means adherence to a set of values at variance with those of the general society; rather, it means a stronger and more explicitly religious affirmation of the same values held by the community at large.[1]

These generalizations ignore significant regional, cultural and religious-cultural diversity in American society, and it is important to recognize that in America, as elsewhere in modern industrial societies, certain energetic sectarian and cultic movements have been able largely to resist becoming 'radically voided' of specifically 'religious' contents. Yet the general trend has been vital, for the bulk of the churchgoing population and the mainstream American religious traditions have been caught up in it, and dominated by it. It would, in short, be hard to oppose Thomas Luckmann's contention that the role of religion in the cultural, social and psychological life of modern America would, 'in the view the churches traditionally held of themselves', have to be considered 'secular' rather than 'religious'.

In British Christianity the same tendencies manifested themselves rather differently. Institutional secularization in the wider society has advanced more rapidly than in America, and the residuum of 'religious terminology' and formal Christianity is therefore less conspicuous, less authentic, less seriously regarded. The public forms of 'religion-in-general' are no longer, in most areas of British society, obligatory conventions of respectability and propriety. Hence while both cultures have been largely secularized, institutional religion is better patronized in the United States than in Britain; and, conversely, within the various British Christian traditions the evacuation of 'religious contents', with its accompanying emergence of a more or less undifferentiated 'common faith', has progressed less rapidly.

A vital difference between the secularization of the 'Church' and the secularization of the wider culture is that the involvement of the Churches in the former process is to a significant extent *active* as well as simply *reactive*. As the distinction between accommodation and resistance implies, there are choices available to the Christian community in the post-Christian environment. There are divergent strategies to be considered. Yet while such choices are real, they are not really free choices. It is a mistake to see the Christian decision-makers and their churchgoing clients as detached observers considering how to deal with a secular world, for they themselves are part of that world. They occupy positions which drift, perhaps imperceptibly, with secular currents. Their manoeuvring within these currents may be skillful or inept, perceptive or short-sighted, important or inconsequential. But manoeuvres, strategies and tactics are conscious things, and before considering the conscious developments, it is important to recognize how much the evacuation of 'religious contents' from modern Christian culture has been simply an inevitable extension, into the Churches, of the secularization of the social order in which its leaders and members spend their lives.

## SECULARIZATION AND THE LAITY

Like all voluntary associations, modern Churches are in large measure what their rank-and-file members make them. The beliefs, values and intensity of commitment found in the pews, however inchoate, slight or theologically unedifying, help to shape a denominational culture and determine how it evolves. Hence the importance of the fact that in the past 100 years the British pew has become a point of infiltration for secular influences. With apt timing, the Presidential Address to British Wesleyans marking the opening of the twentieth century included the observation: 'You are in the world, brethren, steeped in its affairs, conversant with its ideas, and affected by its fashions and maxims to a degree that would have shocked your fathers'.[2] Precisely the same remarks might have been addressed equally well to a majority in any of the major denominations: the twentieth-century Christian was also a citizen of an increasingly secular society, a participant in an increasingly areligious culture.

One effect of this dual involvement was the appearance among Christians of ideas and assumptions whose essential secularity inevitably affected the spirit of traditional doctrines, if not always (or immediately) their actual credal statement. The once-sectarian Nonconformist denominations bore the most obvious signs of this subtle ideological secularization, but no religious culture escaped it. As early as the final quarter of the nineteenth century the leading Congregational theologian, R. W. Dale, could speak of the less palatable elements of traditional orthodoxy – the doctrines of Hell, Atonement, Biblical Inspiration, etc – being 'silently relegated, with or without very serious consideration, to that province of the intellect which is the home of beliefs which have not been rejected, but which we are willing to forget'.[3] Among the Methodists Hugh Price Hughes, a minister well placed to observe such trends, detected 'an unhealthy softening of the fibres of faith', and felt that 'men do not believe so heartily and emphatically as they once did'.[4] And C. H. Spurgeon, Baptist contemporary of Dale and Hughes, but rather more conservative theologically than either, made the same point more strongly, and opposed with grim determination the relaxation of standards *within* the circles of formal orthodoxy.

Ordinary Christian believers were, for the first time, being forced into unconscious compromise by the passing of the traditional 'religious *a priori*'. 'They cannot hate the unbelievers', a Victorian social critic observed in 1878, 'for they daily live in amity with them; nor despise altogether their judgment, for the most eminent thinkers of the day belong to them.' He pointed out that 'even the strongest faith' could not fail to be affected under such circumstances. 'It may not lose its firmness, but it must lose something of its fervour . . . .'.[5] In all the Churches, as the twentieth century has passed, belief has been secularized in this way; and the resulting tolerant climate has permitted explicit attacks on credal othodoxy to go almost uncensured. Professor G. W. H. Lampe, an Anglican theologian, made the point, during a Convocation debate in 1974, that Anglican attitudes to traditional doctrines had evolved a 'remarkable pluralism'. Few, he suggested, would doubt the literal truth of 'was crucified' and 'buried', and none would take literally the phrase 'sitteth on the right hand of God the Father',

but as far as the other two terms, 'He rose from the dead, ascended into heaven', there would be great variety, even among those who use the Creeds and repeat them *ex animo*, about where literal history and where symbolism begin and end.[6]

It would of course be foolish to assume that the average man-in-the-pew has *ever* been an informed and literal believer in credal orthodoxies. Equally, however, it is scarcely plausible that the beliefs and assumptions of British Christianity have not, in the modern world, been rationalized and secularized partly by influences operating below the level of pulpit and seminary. In 1970 a Harris Poll on 'The Religious Beliefs of the British People' discovered that in the Church of England, and the Catholic and Methodist Churches, the majority of ordinary members felt that religion should 'Adapt to the modern world' rather than 'Keep to traditional forms'.[7] Two years earlier, of respondents claiming to be 'fairly religious' when questioned about their beliefs by the Opinion Research Centre, half had admitted to thinking of God merely as 'Some kind of impersonal power'; and even among the 'strongly religious', only 60 per cent had expressed belief in a personal God.[8] Such opinion-sampling evidence has been confirmed by numerous Church leaders. In a considered comment following discussions at the Birmingham Church Leaders Conference of 1972, for example, John Macquarrie, a prominent Anglican theologian, noted widespread Christian 'bewilderment' over questions about 'God' and 'prayer'. 'The sources of this bewilderment are complex', he said, but 'certainly one cannot blame a few *avant-garde* theologians for upsetting people's beliefs'.[9]

The theology of the pew has thus grown more 'secular', less inclined towards supernaturalism and other-worldly consciousness. And the same can be said for the values and norms governing conventional Christian behaviour. As religion has become a segmental activity in modern society, with denominational associations representing merely one involvement among many for people moving in a pluralistic, differentiated social environment, it has lost its traditional, normative role over social life generally. At the same time, moreover, it has had to compete for the support of individuals with secular habits of mind and behaviour made possible and legitimate by this very eclipse of religious sanctions! To recruit and retain adherents in such circumstances has meant that the Churches have been forced into continual compromise, A denomination accepts fairly minimal commitment as the price it must pay for quantitatively significant influence in its society, and the concomitant of minimal commitment is minimal differentiation between the churchgoer and the non-churchgoer. This dilemma of the 'Church' in a secular 'world' becomes, in short, the source from which 'worldly' influences can operate within a religious culture to erode traditional Christian taboos, ethics and moral standards.

A sectarian sub-culture can resist such secularization; a denomination, with its client relationship to the wider culture, ultimately is unable to do so. Late nineteenth-century British denominationalism was well aware of the danger. Running parallel to the theological controversies which accompanied the secularization of popular beliefs, the late Victorian and Edwardian periods saw determined rearguard actions against signs of a creeping 'worldliness' in Christian communities. Like the famous theological controversies over Darwinism, Biblican Criticism, Christology and Eschatology, the battle against worldliness proceeded at different speeds and with different kinds of preoccupations from denomination to denomination. The general trend was the same, however. Churches which once had fulminated against secular novels and frivolous conversation, and pronounced anathema on the card table, dance-hall or theatre, ended up seeing nothing essentially wrong with any of these things. All habits, institutions and activities accepted as legitimate by majority public opinion were, in the long run, sanctioned by denominational Christianity. And if the Churches can still claim to be influencing the ethical standards of the 'world', what is more obvious is that worldly standards have become, in the modern period, the arbiters of Christian ethics.

A conspicuous result of the change, as Chapter Four has argued, has been the secularization of Sunday, even for those who spare a weekend hour to practise religion. But other aspects of religious practice have also declined as a result of secularization's impact on the-man-in-the-pew. The most demanding forms of practice had been the first to feel the pressure. The decline of the once-mandatory Methodist Class Meeting was virtually complete by 1900. Attendance at Class formerly had been the basis of membership; in the previous half-century, however, it had become first optional, then increasingly unpopular. In other denominations week-night meetings were in the process of similar decline around 1900. The *Daily News* carried out a careful religious census of London in 1903, and discovered not only that just one in ten Sunday churchgoers also attended week-night meetings, but that when ancillary activities did continue to attract significant numbers they were usually those of a purely social kind: choral societies, popular lectures, church-sponsored Working-Men's Clubs, Pleasant Sunday Afternoons and similar things.[10]

The generalization does not apply equally to all denominations, however. Many Baptists continued to place great store by week-night prayer and Bible-reading meetings during the period when members of other bodies were turning their backs on such things. When in the 1890s and early 1900s first Charles Booth in his massive sociological study of London, and then Mudie-Smith in his analysis of the *Daily News* census data, discovered that Methodists, Presbyterians and (to an even greater extent) Congregationalists, were well on the way to confining 'worship' and 'public piety' to a single Sunday service, Baptist religious culture remained much less secularized. Baptists, in short, have been noticeably slower to reach accommodations with the secular culture, and among them the alternative strategy of resistance has always attracted substantial support.

The more evangelical Anglican fellowships within the Established Church occupied a position comparable, in some respects, with that of the Baptists within English Nonconformity. In general, however, institutional secularization was as evident in the National Church as elsewhere. When invited in 1903 to describe 'The ideal church for East London', for example, an Anglican leader gave the *Daily News* investigators the following outline: a spacious building with a good organ, a platform instead of a pulpit, adjacent class rooms and games rooms, a number of associated 'clubs' catering for gymnastics, athletics and music, and an active social programme including 'At Homes' sponsored by individual families, weekend rambles and museum visits, Saturday night concerts and popular lectures, a maternity club, a Loan and Sickness Benefit Society, and secular educational services of various kinds.

This is an interesting catalogue proposing a comprehensive involvement of the parish church in local urban community life. Comprehensive involvement had been characteristic of religion in the cohesive, total communities of the pre-industrial world, so the aspiration was traditional. But the circumstances and methods of the early twentieth century were novel. Traditional social activities once monopolized by the Churches could now be catered for by purely secular institutions and organizations covering such things as sport, recreation, social welfare, education and entertainment. As a *basic* institution in its own right, the Church had been able to use its involvement in these things to sacralize them; but once forced to rely on secular functions to retain popular support, the modern Church was secularized by them. The evident secularity and low-level commitment of the ordinary churchgoer presented religious organizations with the alternatives of accommodation or loss of public patronage, for people with numerous 'serving institutions' to choose from sat loose to religious services and ministerial demands which seemed onerous, prescriptive or dull. In the 'market situation' of competing denominations and increasingly reluctant 'consumers', modern religion, chameleon-like, unconsciously took the colour and texture of its social environment. As a candid Independent scholar put it in 1898, 'Not for long does a minister address himself to reluctant hearers; no voice of duty bids them endure when worship becomes difficult'.[12]

Declining attendance and membership thus failed to mirror the full impact of secularization not only, as Chapter Four has shown, because it was accompanied by a debilitating transition from allogenous to autogenous growth, but also because the commitment demanded by membership was becoming increasingly minimal. Secularization within the 'Church' thus delayed the full realization of institutional secularization in the society as a whole. The decline of ecclesiastical discipline provides perhaps the most blatant example of this process. Fear of 'the flesh, the world and the devil' is, of course, as old as Christianity itself, and however ascetic a religious culture there is always room for a hard line against alleged breaches of discipline and commitment. But as the intensity went out of denominational commitment, discipline was something the Churches could ill-afford in the struggle to attract and retain support.

As its Class Meeting declined, for example, Methodism lost both its most effective instrument for exacting compliance with traditional Methodist norms, and its primary method of demanding of members a more than perfunctory level of commitment. Similarly, as the once-normative 'Church Meeting' lost significance in Independent polity (a process well advanced in both Congregationalist and Baptist circles by 1914), the situation emerged in which people could retain membership simply because, as one observer put it, there was 'no overt reason, known to the Executive, why they should be dropped'.[13] 'Expulsion' or 'ex-communication' had been an essential fact of Nonconformist life in the eighteenth and early nineteenth centuries, and some denominations came to consider it of sufficient quantitative importance to begin keeping separate statistical series relating losses by 'expulsion' to overall losses.

Such series measure declining standards of discipline and, less directly, of commitment, although in most cases their central collation and publication actually began after the process of internal secularization had set in. In the Presbyterian Church of Wales, for example, annual 'expulsions', running between 750 and 850 per annum in the 1890s, actually rose at the time of the great 'Welsh Revival' to 1,292 in 1905, but thereafter the downward trend (which probably started at least as early as 1880), was resumed. By 1955 'expulsions' had fallen to just 52, and two years later the Church simply dropped the series altogether. The intervening trend indicated that while decline was going on throughout the period after 1905, it was during and after World War II that denominational discipline suffered its greatest collapse. Annual 'expulsions' were still running at around 350-400 per year until the 1930s, but in 1939 the figure dropped to 200, and the annual average for the 1940s was below 180.[14]

If this was a typical Nonconformist pattern, in the Church of England discipline has never, in modern times, been sufficiently strong to provide for effective ex-communication. Indeed, Anglicanism was the first religious culture to offer the English people what has been called scathingly 'cheap grace': a religion demanding minimal commitment, and requiring neither deviation from the generally-accepted ethical and social standards of the wider society nor burdensome donations of time, money or energy. Probably for this reason, its twentieth-century decline has been less obvious in participatory terms than the decline of the modern Free Churches, whose residual strain of sectarian hostility to the 'world' still appears to give religious commitment a certain social cost. Moreover, the secularization of the Establishment gave the *Catholic Times* a ready answer when in 1957 the Anglican Bishop of Lichfield boasted that for every Anglican in his diocese becoming a Catholic, four Catholics were converted to Anglicanism. 'The demands of the Church of England', said the *Catholic Times*,

are not frightfully severe. You can believe practically anything; you have a wide choice of worship; moral standards are not very exacting. Small wonder, then, if there are half-hearted Catholics who lapse into this more comfortable way of life.[15]

The secularization of the Church, then, means, in the final resort, that those tests, standards and patterns of behaviour defining boundaries between the 'Church' and the 'world' have become less and less discernible, and that the 'cost' of Christian commitment has been correspondingly devalued. Today denominational religion is little more than one of a growing number of equally legitimate leisure-time pursuits, one of a range of recreational cultures in a situation of cultural pluralism. As W. S. F. Pickering has observed: 'If the "cost" is persecution or death, the practice of religion is hardly equivalent to membership of a gardening club! If on the other hand the "cost" is minimal, religion may be assumed to be lightly esteemed'.[16] The foregoing analysis has not presumed that genuine religious commitment was uniformly high in the past, or implied that intense commitment is entirely lacking in the modern Churches, but it has sought to establish that since the late nineteenth century the British Churches have been progressively secularized partly by the increasingly secular values, assumptions and expectations characteristic of ordinary Christian lay people.

## SECULARIZATION AND THE MINISTRY

While denominational laymen have 'leavened' modern British Christianity with their growing secularity, responsibility for secularization within the Churches also rests partly with the professional ministry. Indeed, as the history of ecumenism, the liberalization of theology and the relaxation of ecclesiastical discipline confirms, it is the ministry which usually has taken the lead in efforts to accommodate Christianity to the modern world. Secularization places the ministry in a particularly invidious position. While there can be no doubt about the integrity of ministerial behaviour in most cases, it is naive not to recognize that a professional ministry faces a very difficult crisis of 'mixed motivation' in a situation of serious and prolonged organizational decline. The laity, only segmentally committed to the declining institution, dependent more on the 'world' than the 'Church' for status, economic security and even social satisfactions, have less to lose, in mundane terms, through secularization. The professional minister has everything to lose: income, status, security, and that vital cluster of human needs sometimes encompassed by the term 'job satisfaction.'

A century-and-a-half ago the Anglican ministry was still the most prestigious of all professions in British society, and for many aspirants probably the most lucrative and secure. That this seems incredible today is a measure of the cultural and institutional secularization which has occurred. The Nonconformist pastorate was also highly regarded within the social strata from which it drew its members, and entry into the ministerial profession, for Church and chapel alike, usually meant an enhancement of status for the individual concerned. The man in the pulpit could expect to be better educated, and in the widest sense, more cultured, than the great majority of his congregation. By the end of the nineteenth century, however, concern about the growing scarcity of 'gentlemen' ordinands in the Church of England was becoming widespread, and competing professional opportunities were depleting the numbers and quality of candidates in all the Churches. As the Bishop of Lincoln put it somewhat quaintly in 1901, 'the hero of the modern schoolboy is not connected with the ministerial life as it was formerly'.[17]

Schoolboys are realistic about such matters. While the standard of living of the Victorian middle classes had risen very appreciably, clerical incomes had declined, in real terms, by about a third.[18] The decline of status had been even more marked. The proportion of Anglican bishops drawn from the peerage had contracted sharply; the proportion of magistrates drawn from the clergy, a good measure of the social status of the profession, had been higher in 1830 than ever before, but by the final quarter of the century it had fallen to an almost insignificant level;[19] the Vestry Meeting had lost its traditional role as a central institution in the ordering of local communities in rural England, certainly after the Local Government Act of 1894; and, as a cultural consequence of such trends, there was a crisis of social confidence throughout the Anglican ministry. The country parson, in Owen Chadwick's words, seemed 'somehow less easy in society, less like ordinary gentlemen . . . '.[20] It can scarcely be wondered at that by the end of the Victorian era the medical profession, the law, the civil service and the world of business had all surpassed the clerical life in appeal to the well-educated, well-connected young men leaving the public schools.[21]

In some respects, of course, this was no bad thing. Its inescapable aura of gentility had been a millstone around the neck of the Victorian Church in its ministrations to the masses of working and lower-middle-class people. 'Go among the poor as much as he may', D. C. Pedder wrote in 1906, 'the clergyman of the Church of England is nothing more than a diver who takes his atmosphere with him. That is the only way he can breath when he has left his own element, and his element is gentility'.[22] The Church needed a new kind of ministry, he concluded: it had to find ordinands from among the 'common people'. But the story of the twentieth century has been one of failure to effect any radical transformation of the social character of the clergy. While the 'Paul Report' of 1964 was able to trace a slight movement away from the traditional bias in favour of landed families and the upper middle class, it expressed the fear that the 'urban millions' might still easily 'form the impression that by class and accent the Church, and its ministry, are no more for them than the Royal Enclosure at Goodwood'.[23]

The modern Anglican clergyman thus has the worst of both worlds: the social and cultural values, norms, learning, experience and expectations of gentility to distance him from the bulk of his parishioners, and simultaneously the grave problem of a stipend far too low to allow him to maintain the material standards appropriate to professional social status. It is a far cry from the Goodwood Royal Enclosure to the domestic realities of young wives working full time out of economic necessity, and leaving 'father, the vicar', to get children to school and do the household chores. The mixture of new economic problems and traditional social expectations produces obvious tensions. One parson told Leslie Paul in 1963: 'The chief thing which vitiates my work is the continual dread of failing to make ends meet . . . ' Most, replying to the same questionnaire, agreed that £850-00 per annum fell well short of essential expenditure; and in a somewhat pathetic mixture of social snobbery and professional demoralization, another, reporting 'great sacrifices' financially, explained:

Living in a country village with an entirely peasant-type population meant no friends for my children. Hence the expense of a nursery school (£22-00 per term), travelling twelve miles daily by car. This was a necessity now they are of school age. I do not wish them to be subjected to the anti-Church atmosphere of the village school and to share in our own persecution. I feel I ought to send them to a private school.[24]

A rather unedifying, utterly inevitable conclusion to the economic decline of the clerical profession has been the recent emergence, among Anglican clergy, of what amounts to industrial action. Some have joined secular trade unions, others have placed their faith in a representative professional body for the clergy designed specifically to 'negotiate with central Church authorities matters relating to . . . pay and conditions'. The attitude of this Association of the Clergy, stated in a circular letter which received front-page publicity in the *Church Times* in 1977, is that,

Quite bluntly, the Church is grossly exploiting many of its full-time employees; besides its injustice, this is bound to affect the calibre of men offering themselves for the full-time ministry.[25]

As if to confirm this sombre view, in the week following publication of the Association's circular the appearance of an official report by the Archbishop of Canterbury on *The Ordained Ministry Today and Tomorrow* warned that a continuing decline in the number of candidates for Holy Orders had become so serious that Anglicanism faced a crisis of 'considerable magnitude'. Indeed, the Archbishop foresaw 'a downward spiral: fewer priests serving scattered and declining congregations, with fewer people to provide a stipendary ministry and even less money available for training and stipends'.[26] A considerable crisis indeed!

And other Churches faced the same crisis. In 1971 the Congregational pastor of Kensington Chapel, Alec Gilmore, agreed with the conclusion of a fellow minister: 'We are witnessing the disappearance of a profession, but cannot bring ouselves to admit it'.[27] Another Congregationalist, Ernest Marvin, pointed out in the same study that in 1971 even £1,000-00 per annum, which only the Church of Scotland and the Church of England could hope to offer their ministers, was not a viable stipend. Ministers of religion were a profession living below the 'poverty line', Marvin insisted. He admitted to having met a number of Free Church ministers, as well as certain well-paid laymen, who felt that ministerial stipends were adequate; but of the former he remarked wryly that, 'on the lamented demise of two of them, I discovered that they each had a private income'.[28]

Growing economic hardship and consequently diminishing social status would be enough to produce demoralization in the most dedicated profession, but in the case of ministers of religion this demoralization has been exacerbated by doubts about the relevance and legitimacy of their primary professional functions. The ministry is a unique profession, involving what the sociologist, Eric Carlton, has called 'institutionalized ambiguity'. Discussing the mixed motivation inherent in the 'call' to a Baptist or Congregationalist pastorate, Carlton has explained that:

The stipend, the membership, the manse, free Sundays, schools for the children – all these are important in any consideration of 'call', but ministers insist that these are externalities, and do not fully explain *why* men make the decisions they do. They testify to hours spent in prayer, and may Mosaically look for a few modest 'signs', disregarding the dangers of self-congratulatory fulfilments.[29]

Both aspects of this complex motivation are affected by secularization. If the status, remuneration and security of the clergy declines as the wider society becomes less supportive, the confidence of the clergyman (or prospective clergyman) in the relevance and legitimacy of his role is sapped by the prevailing secular outlook which he cannot easily ignore or totally reject.

The main 'turmoil' in the contemporary ministry may well be essentially spiritual, and almost certainly it has more to do with *role* than *remuneration*. Psychiatrists, social workers, educators and entertainers have steadily usurped roles once reserved to the clergy, but there is a deeper problem. Among Christian ministers 'modern life' has brought, in the words of a leading Baptist pastor, 'the deepening sense that even the "proper" work of the ministry fails to connect with the reality either of God or of man, that it has become a meaningless masquerade, that it has suffered an almost total evacuation of significance'.[30] The Scottish Churchman and theologian, Nevile Davidson, has identified precisely the same root cause of the 'tragic shortage of clergy' available to Scottish Presbyterianism.[31]

Various modern ecclesiastical tendencies can be interpreted partly as responses to this complex crisis facing the professional ministry. One is the strong emphasis in many sections of modern Christianity on liturgical aspects of faith. In a world of theological scepticism, professional social work and secular psychiatry, the minister of religion presumably can count on an unchallenged monopoly of sacramental functions. Thus the Baptist, Neville Clark, noting the 'role confusion' of the modern minister, has gone on to argue that it is 'in liturgical assembly that the shaping of the ministerial task takes place.' In a vein typical of numerous modern discussions of the ministry, his analysis has called for a stronger emphasis on the meaning, importance and centrality of liturgy, and has concluded that to sever any other part of the minister's work from this its 'ultimate ground' is to doom it, finally, to 'irrelevancy'.[32] In somewhat more lyrical prose David Jenkins, Anglican clergyman, philosopher and ecumenical leader, has expanded this point. Christian social services, although 'a ministry within the care of God', actually require neither clergy nor hallowed buildings, he has observed; but an ordained ministry does have a special, unique duty

to be the focus of the people who cherish the salt of the knowledge of God, tend the flame of the challenge of the transcendent and refuse to lose sight of the prophetic and the mysterious.[33]

A look at both the arguments and the advocates favouring liturgical renewal confirms that it cannot be dismissed simply as an escapist effort to retreat into a kind of cultic role which is rendered secure by its very irrelevance or triviality. Certain liturgical controversies and obsessions do, admittedly, have this 'neurotic nature',[34] but the same can be said of any other development within the modern ministry. Convocation has been warned on several occasions that, for certain clergymen, specialized social ministries, such as hospital or prison chaplaincies, can themselves be a form of 'escapism' for ministries unsure about the significance or legitimacy of their uniquely 'religious' functions. But the basic inspiration favouring liturgical renewal has, in fact, been a concern to deepen the impact of the 'Church' on the 'world'. Thus a typical modern understanding of the Eucharist emphasises that it is the celebration of the world's redemption. It is the effective re-enactment of the reconciling travail of God with his creation, and therefore the unmasking of the cross and resurrection in the midst of life, time and history. To celebrate the supper is to set the congregation at the focal point of judgment and renewal, that thereby it may be hurled afresh into the ongoing mission of the Lord.[35]

But here, too, there is evidence of accommodation. Indeed, it is with evident relief that the theologian adumbrating such a view of the Eucharist can conclude that the ministerial celebrant is performing 'the most profoundly secular act that, in this life, men are given to do'.[36]

Secularity becomes a clerical virtue in the accommodatory exercise. Quite apart from particular aspects of the ministerial role, many clergymen evidently are almost as uneasy, diffident and readily embarrassed about the specifically 'religious' demands of their office as many modern lay people seem to be. When in the mid-1960s Robert Towler conducted a sample study of Anglican ordinands, he discovered a basic division which matches the distinction between accommodation and resistance. The first group of ordinands, which Towler called *antipuritans*, outnumbered the second, the *puritans*, and in comparison with them seemed essentially 'unreligious'. Ordinands which he classified as puritans seemed to Towler 'to be interested in religion to the exclusion of all else', and to relate 'matters quite unconnected with religion' to 'a religious frame of reference'. Antipuritans, on the other hand, seemed to talk about 'anything but religion'. Their attitudes to their cultic activities, to prayer, preaching and church services, 'could best be described as casual', Towler found; and on a sociological test of 'religious interest', as a group they scored little higher than a random sample of the population at large, and 33 per cent lower than the puritan sample. Moreover, in conversation with Towler the antipuritan type emerged as someone who 'frequently finds in the arts and non-religious affairs more interest and "inspiration" than he does in religion', who lacks any 'compelling experience of the supernatural', and who has 'no sense of alienation between the religious and secular spheres'.[37] In terms of churchmanship, antipuritans were by self-definition a mixture of anglo-catholics and liberals; puritans were drawn largely from the evangelical wing of the Church of England.[38]

Evangelicals apart, then, the younger clergy of the Church of England are in large number essentially secular in outlook. They may be religious in the sense that they recognize the pertinence of the basic human questions, Who am I? Who made me? For what purpose? Where am I going? But in the answers which they feel capable of giving they are at one with the secular philosophies of the age. To an older clergyman listening to a long Convocation discussion of 'The Spiritual

Life of the Clergy', the talk about 'meaningful experimentation' and non-religious forms of transcendental meditation meant only one thing:

we are acknowledging that the clergy of the Church of England, by and large, have little or no spiritual life. If this is the case, then we are in a sad position indeed![39]

But what was the alternative? If antipuritans are *unspiritual*, puritans may simply be *unheard* in a secular world. This dilemma of the 'Church' in its modern 'world' is perhaps even more acutely obvious when we turn to the history of theology.


## THE SEARCH FOR A PREACHABLE GOSPEL

Historical theology is among the best-covered areas of religious studies, a field far too developed either to require detailed elaboration, or to be advanced by the kind of analysis possible within the limits of the present broad study. Yet its major trends must be summarized. For the ideological evolution of modern Christianity, more clearly perhaps than any other aspect of the 'Church'–'world' relationship, illuminates the basic dilemma posed by secularization. This is because modern theologians have been motivated chiefly by the crisis of plausibility confronting orthodox transcendental theology in a secular culture. As Reginald W. Thompson, Chairman of the Congregational Union of England and Wales in 1938, put it in an official address to his denomination, 'A true Gospel must be preachable.' The Congregationalists, he remarked somewhat sweepingly,

have abandoned doctrines once thought essential: physical hell; total depravity; endless punishment for sins committed in this moment of life; Christ *punished* by God for other's sins; the predestination of some to eternal woe. Not all these dogmas were, I fancy, abandoned under pressure of abstract theological studies, but because the working minister found they simply could not be told as Good News to the people. *A true Gospel must be preachable.*[40]

Congregationalist ministers in fact came rather late to this criterion. The original conception of modern liberal theology, Friedrick Schleiermacher's *On Religion – Speeches to its Cultured Despisers,* had begun the search for a preachable Gospel as early as 1799. Schleiermacher had been concerned to so adapt theology that it could appeal to an areligious audience – the 'cultured despisers'. And because modern secular consciousness would never accord Christianity the same 'level of certainty' as science or social theory, he had tried to evolve a faith so essentially subjective as to resign 'all claims on anything that belongs either to science or morality.' Too radical for most of his Christian contemporaries, Schleiermacher's approach nevertheless became a blueprint for many later developments of liberal Protestantism. It was, in particular, frankly accommodatory in spirit. After Schleiermacher it was the beliefs and assumptions of secular intellectuals, not, in Berger's words, 'the sources of his own tradition', which would 'serve the Protestant theologian as arbiters of cognitive acceptability'.[41]

The nineteenth century saw this liberal approach make gradual inroads into traditional orthodoxy, a process which accompanied the rise of secular humanism in Britain. The search was for a Gospel 'preachable', in the first instance, to church members, secondarily to the internal constituencies of sympathizers and attached adolescents, and ultimately to a secular 'world'. With German Biblical Criticism often pointing the way (especially after 1846, when Marianne Evans gave readers of English a translation of Strauss's *Das Leben Jesu*), and with the impact of Darwinian science stimulating popular concern about the need for rapprochement between religious and secular knowledge, the second half of the nineteenth century saw liberal theology loosening the grip of evangelical orthodoxy on British Protestantism. The tide ebbed and flowed. An eminent Anglican theologian, F. D. Maurice, lost his professional position at King's College, London, in 1853, after publicly questioning the doctrine of eternal damnation, but seven years later the equally controversial *Essays and Reviews* survived criticism, to enhance rather than retard the ecclesiastical careers of its authors. In October 1877 Congregationalists were scandalized by the airing of advanced liberal views at the Autumnal Meeting of their Union, held in Leicester; thirty years later, however, J. R. Campbell's, *The New Theology*, became, in J. W. Grant's words, 'a decisive point in the history of Nonconformist churchmanship'. It brought 'extreme liberalism' into the open, especially at the influential level of theological college curricula, and assured modern theological tendencies a permanent legitimacy within the denomination.

Modernism, as the pre-1914 liberal theology was called, foundered under the impact of the First World War, along with other forms of naively optimistic humanism. But it was not traditional evangelical orthodoxy which led the post-war reaction against the modernists, it was the 'neo-orthodoxy' of Karl Barth, Reinhold Neibuhr and others. And this Barthian reaction, with a deep scepticism of all traditional 'religious' assumptions, soon generated new radical theological quests just as surely as it stultified the old superficialities of modernism. By the end of the Second World War it had spawned a new, variegated liberalism. Bultmann's 1941 lecture, 'New Testament and Mythology', almost immediately re-directed much theological enterprise towards an existentialist understanding of Christianity, and by 1950 it was Bultmann, not Barth, whose ideas were at the centre of Protestant theological debate.

With Bultmann, moreover, the original Schleiermachian concern to adapt the Gospel to a modern secular culture had once more become primary. Nor was Bultmann alone in this re-assertion. The same concern lay at the heart of Bonhoeffer's attenuated efforts to construct a 'religionless Christianity'. For it was against a background shaped by secularization that he sought to interpret the sacred 'in a worldly manner' and wrestled with the question, 'How can Christ become the Lord even of those of no Religion?'[42] Meanwhile, a third member of this influential generation, Paul Tillich, went even further than either Bultmann or Bonhoeffer 'in trying to give the Christian faith an expression which will render it intelligible to men of the world, while preserving its unique substance'.[43] Reading Tillich may suggest that he expected rather too much erudition from the 'men of the world', and discovered rather too little substance in Christian theology, but his work was in the vanguard of the theology of accommodation, and this alone guaranteed its significance.

British theology followed these developments, and rarely broke new ground, for the leading British scholars tended to be in the field of New Testament studies rather than systematic or philosophical theology. But in 1963, in a brilliantly-orchestrated publishing triumph, John A. T. Robinson, then Bishop of Woolwich, gave the British public a short, simplified account of where the new liberalism was leading. In *Honest to God*, without being entirely fair to any of his sources, Robinson borrowed ideas from Bultmann, Bonhoeffer and Tillich to construct a single, coherent case for re-thinking the concept of 'God'. The work was a massive success for its publishers. It sold more copies, more quickly, 'than any new book of serious theology in the history of the world',[44] and prompted a flood of reviews, reactions, television and radio broadcasts, cartoons and sermons.

The appearance of *Honest to God* was a vital event in the making of post-Christian Britain. It precipitated attitudes towards religion which long had remained in suspension – vague, inchoate, undecided. It confronted 'Church' and 'world' alike. Minds were made up. Tenuous links were broken. It is impossible, a decade-and-a-half later, not to conclude that the publication hastened the decline of British Christianity and actually increased the estrangement from the secular culture of that waning religious tradition which the Bishop sought to make more preachable. The period since the early 1960s has seen a marked de-mobilization of denominational constituencies, as well as increasing rates of defection from the ranks of existing members. It has at the same time seen a growing willingness within the wider society for people actually to admit their unbelief. Many factors have been involved, but at the level of consciousness *Honest to God*, and the debates it generated, almost certainly was an important catalyst.

When B. Seebohm Rowntree and G. R. Lavers conducted 200 in-depth interviews prior to publishing *English Life and Leisure* in 1951, they discovered a very common attitude towards religion which might be called *cognitive acquiesence*. Its hallmark was negligible commitment coupled with a nominal acceptance of prevailing beliefs and social habits. Of a typical interviewee Rowntree and Lavers reported: 'Has never thought much about the basic dogma of Christianity. Everybody accepted it so he did, and he supposes he still does'.[45] Obviously, this kind of cognitive acquiesence is a fragile basis for a religious culture. Any dramatic contradiction arising from personal experience can destroy it totally in the case of an individual; but even more importantly, from a social viewpoint, anything precipitating public reappraisal of the conventional wisdom, anything shaking the kaleidoscope of habit, assumption and received opinion, creates a new cultural situation. *Honest to God* shook the kaleidoscope. In a letter typical of many received by Robinson immediately after the book appeared, a former churchgoer remarked bitterly, 'now the parsons are contradicting everything they have said'; and asked whether, if 'everything they have taught us is wrong, how can they be right as to what they tell us now'? In similar vein, an Anglican priest paraphrased a common public reaction as follows:

Well, I've always said it's difficult to believe in a God who allows all this suffering and misery that goes on in the world – and now, see – a bishop tells us we needn't believe in God at all – nor go to church. He says religion isn't necessary – it's all phoney; all we need do is to lead decent lives and be kind to others.[46]

Theologians and philosophers made the same kind of point. E. L. Mascall, Professor of historical theology at London University, agreed with Robinson's insistence that Christianity must be made 'relevant to modern man', but only if 'this means persuading secular man that he must no longer be merely secular'. For if, on the other hand, the truth really was, in the Bishop's words, that 'God is teaching us that we must live as men who can get on very well without him', then, Mascall suggested somewhat wryly, 'the Church has no need to say anything whatever to secularized man, for that is precisely what secularized man already believes'.[47] The non-Christian philosopher, Alasdair MacIntyre, was even more candid. He opened a review in *Encounter* with the words: 'What is striking about Dr. Robinson's book is first and foremost that he is an atheist'.[48]

MacIntyre proceeded in this *Encounter* article to identify the inescapable dilemma of modern theology. Maintaining traditional orthodoxy meant losing intellectual contact with a secular culture, and entering a 'closed circle, in which believer speaks only to believer'. Hence the mainstream response of a theological radicalism in search of a preachable Gospel: 'Turning aside from this arid in-group theology', said MacIntyre,

the most perceptive theologians wish to translate what they have to say to an atheistic world. But they are doomed to one of two failures. Either they succeed in the translation: in which case what they find themselves saying has been transformed into the atheism of their hearers. Or they fail in their translation: in which case no one hears what they have to say but themselves.[49]

Theology has not stood still since 1963, but the impact of *Honest to God*, like the impact of *Essays and Reviews* a century earlier, has clarified the relationship between the contemporary 'Church' and the modern 'world'. Denominational Christianity, responding to secularization essentially by accommodation, had conducted a century-long search – through adaptations, deletions, and reinterpretations designed to make Christianity intelligible and relevant to secular consciousness – for a theology which the world could hear and understand. At last, for a short period in 1963, communication was achieved. The 'Honest to God' debate captured the attention of the British public. But what was left to communicate? There was little that was offensive, unintelligible or mysterious, little to confuse the secular mind; little, indeed, of anything at all. Attempts to make the Gospel 'preachable' seemed to have made it simply vacuous – or at least to have reduced it to the level of an ethical system with which few secular observers would disagree, but with which few would feel any need to make any nominal identification. Thus the secularization of theology passed the point beyond which there is simply no powerful ideological reason for calling people out of the 'world' into a denominational 'Church'.

## THE SECULAR CHURCH MILITANT

More accurately, perhaps, there is no powerful 'religious' reason for issuing such a call. For the accommodation of the 'Church' to the 'world' does not necessarily mean an identification of Christianity with the social or political status quo in a secular society. Indeed, the reverse is often true. An inescapable fact of recent religious history in Western culture has been a correlation between the impact of secularization and the vogue of 'left-liberal' thinking amongst certain theologians and church leaders. On a range of touchstone issues like race, poverty, capital punishment, capitalism and, often enough, even homosexuality and radical feminism, a large and vocal section of the modern Churches has adopted positions which some observers have called 'trendy', but which the liberal religious intelligentsia prefers to think of as 'prophetic'.

The left-liberal clergyman, minister or priest is the modern Christian militant. He has a solution to the quest for 'relevance' in the face of secularization. He has a mission to the world. He wants to confront his society, to challenge its complacency, to influence its consciousness – and he succeeds! A world which is indifferent to spiritual homilies and other-worldly consolations sits up and takes notice of World Council of Churches' aid to Patriotic Front guerrillas; and if the reaction is one of horrified denunciation, so much the better, for it is evidence that the church has found a new way to be 'the salt of the earth'. The fact remains, however, that such success is an essentially 'secular' triumph.

In the first place, there is an almost studied secularity about the kind of churchmanship which accompanies Protestant political activism of a left-liberal variety. 'In conference they look like protest-minded dons', the *Observer* remarked of such members of the 1978 Lambeth Conference. 'There are more jeans than cassocks. One American wears a striped English rugby jersey, which is fashionable on campus here. At the last plenary, one arrived with tennis rackets. It gives a certain air of realism to their deliberations.'[50] Presumably, there was also a nicely-judged profanity about the informal conversation of such churchmen, for in a secular world it is the 'profane' which is real, not the 'sacred'.

Secondly, even when identified with a radical minority in national or international politics, left-liberal Protestantism still represents an accommodation so extreme as to amount to a kind of de-christianization from within. However laudable, being denigrated or even persecuted for adopting an unpopular position on secular politics is not especially 'religious'. Being 'fools for Christ's sake' had been the apostolic form of Christian eccentricity; being execrable for aiding liberation movements is, to say the least, a highly secularized equivalent. The transition is nevertheless readily understandable. 'Once theologians are deprived of faith they turn to hope, and hope frustrated converts to politics. . .', David Martin has pointed out recently. 'When God ceases to be transcendent he is re-embodied in the community and the future, more especially the community which marches forward into the future. Jesus becomes the teacher of this community, and is recast either as a hippy preacher or as a zealous revolutionary sympathizer.'[51]

But theologians who have proclaimed 'the death of God' find it difficult to sustain a coherent 'prophetic' role in the name of Christianity. The lure of left-wing politics is understandable enough. Not only does it offer the prospect of high moral commitment in the interests of social justice for the poor, powerless and dispossessed, but it becomes a *raison d'être* for a Church highly secularized. It promises that Christians who are no longer pilgrims looking for another world can regard themselves nevertheless as 'the salt of the earth'. The problem, of course, is that while left-liberal Protestantism, as a political ideology, has no theoretical mooring which is distinctively 'religious', its inheritance of residual theological and religious-cultural traditions robs it of secular ideological rigour. Thus Martin can observe bluntly that 'translations of transcendence first arouse euphoria and then deflate and empty the very dynamism they were intended to sustain. They are the fun thing for half a decade and then their proponents have to move on'.[52]

More to the point of the present study, however, is the fact that even where the contribution of the movement to human rights and social justice is utterly beyond dispute, left-liberal Protestantism (or any of its Catholic equivalents), is in no sense an antidote to secularization, or an effective assertion of a 'religious' position in a post-Christian world.


## ECUMENISM AND SECULARIZATION

For many Christians in the modern world it is not political or social alignments, but the essentially ecclesiastical and religious-cultural strategy of ecumenism which seems to offer the best way forward. Indeed, it has become the mainstream response to secularization. Few aspects of the 'Church'-'world' relationship lie within the orbit of ecclesiastical initiatives and policies – but ecumenism is one which does. Where traditional denominational strategies seem outmoded, unproductive, essentially irrelevent, it still can evoke considerable excitement and generate considerable energy. Perhaps an increasingly indifferent world will take fresh notice of a Church able to present a united front, speak with a single voice, and effectively co-ordinate its activities, beliefs and values. The prospect has obvious appeal for numerous reasons, and British Churchmen often speak as if the success or failure of ecumenical initiatives will determine the future of British Christianity. The view of signatories to the ill-fated Anglican-Methodist Unity Scheme of 1968, for example, was that,

To go back on this at the present time would be a major disaster, not merely for the cause of unity, but for the Christian mission itself.[53]

This was typical ecumenical rhetoric, not least because Christians share with other human beings the tendency to stress the critical importance of precisely those matters over which they may reasonably hope to exert some real influence.

It is evident that ecumenical leadership has attracted many of the most dynamic, optimistic, talented and devoted of modern Church leaders, and there can be no denying that ecumenical initiatives are in the vanguard of church life in many denominations, or that the hopes and concerns of many Christians rest largely upon them. In arguing that ecumenism is a response to ecclesiastical weakness and alienation from the wider society, it is important to recognize that much of the impetus towards union in the modern religious climate comes from those very sections of the Churches involved most actively, and confidently, in evangelization – in attempts to re-Christianize a profane world. Such people see unity as a basis for aggressive outreach, not as a defensive mechanism designed to prolong the survival of a waning sub-culture. They seek to transcend their narrow confessional boundaries, which traditionally have differentiated churches and denominations, in the same spirit which encourages them to free theological systems from what they see as the outmoded accretions of distant historical epochs, and for the same reasons which attract them to the kind of 'liturgical renewal' which promises to enhance Christianity's revelance in the modern world. Furthermore, to argue that ecumenism is essentially a response to the decline of organized religion is to oversimplify a complexity of motives and objectives sustaining the movement. A comprehensive history or sociology of ecumenism would have to explore other aspects and describe other perspectives of the subject, including various historical instances of ecumenical activity arising from *progressive* phases of church growth.[54]

Yet the fact remains that modern ecumenism in Britain has been, in Robert Currie's words, 'the product of an ageing religion'.[55] The proponents of unity have worked with different and sometimes contradictory guiding assumptions and expectations. Professional ministers, for example, have tended to greet the prospect of ecumenism on the basis of motives and interests which often have diverged sharply from those of their lay supporters; and opposition to the movement has been correspondingly heterogeneous. But the twin realities of cultural secularization and institutional decline, and the dilemmas they have created for the Churches, have been primarily responsible for shaping the thinking of both advocates and opponents of unity. Thus while the debate over ecumenism brings together most of the major strands in the response of the 'Church' to the modern secular 'world', the underlying issue, in Britain at least, has been whether or not Christianity should meet its contemporary predicament in a spirit of accommodation and compromise. For however legitimate, positive or evangelistic its inspiration and goals, ecumenism, quite simply, is a reductionist strategy involving compromise within the Christian community and accommodation between the religious culture and its secular environment.

Historically, the correlation is clear. Movements towards unity have coincided with mounting evidence of secular apathy outside the Churches and institutional difficulties within. The idea of 'home mission' was mooted at most sessions of Convocation and most Church Congresses throughout the later years of Victoria's reign, and often linked explicitly with concern about the apparent growth of irreligion in British society. The Lambeth Quadrilateral of 1888, stating the basis on which Anglicanism might co-operate with other Christian bodies, was issued at a time when concern about the 'unchurched masses' was at a peak, and when secular meliorism was beginning to assume definite social programmes and organizational stategies – for example, in the Social Democratic Federation, the 'New Unionism' and the ideas of the early Fabians. The World Missionary Conference at Edinburgh in 1910, which gave direct, lasting stimulus to British ecumenism, confirmed the association between the problems of Christianity in non-Christian cultures and the modern inclination towards Church unity. And after the First World War, which had brought to all the Churches grim reminders of powerlessness and cultural isolation, the Lambeth Conference of 1920 issued its famous 'Appeal to All Christian People', calling for a new 'visible unity' of all Christians in order 'that the world might believe'.

Meanwhile, in a series of ecumenical mergers beginning in 1857 with the formation of the United Methodist Free Churches, British Methodism had proceeded far towards the almost comprehensive re-union which was finally accomplished in 1932. During the great century of Methodist expansion, which had begun in 1739 and ended visibly by the 1840s, the movement had proved highly fragmentary.

Intense commitment had produced a proclivity towards conflict over principle and practice alike, while rapid growth had minimized the consequences of schism. But after the final conflict of 1849 it became clear that Methodist growth rates had settled into a more or less permanent pattern of stagnation or decline, and at the same time denominational leaders saw early signs that rank-and-file commitment was becoming segmental, relaxed and conditional. In such a situation Methodist ecumenism was born. As Robert Currie has written in the conclusion to his definitive study of the subject:

Ecumenicalism develops as conflict declines and as religion declines. Failing to recruit, flourishing communities become sluggish, ageing and dispirited. Conversion of manifest success into manifest failure has nowhere been sharper than in Methodism. This change in fortunes has promoted an atmosphere of malaise. As tolerance of persistent decline fails, the organization seeks to replace missing 'frontal' growth from recruitment with 'lateral' growth from amalgamation.[56]

Although still awaiting the kind of treatment Currie has given to Methodist re-union, the re-union of Scottish Presbyterianism, which culminated in 1929 with the merger between the Church of Scotland and the United Presbyterian Church, seems to fit Currie's general hypothesis perfectly.

Since World War II ecumenism has been chiefly inter-denominational. At a time when the decline of Free Church religion in England and Wales had reached the point where laymen and pastors alike were beginning to speculate about its extinction, ecumenism carried evident appeal, expecially for the professional ministry. A layman could write to the *British Weekly*, with an air of equanimity, that

It may be that the Free Churches have fulfilled their functions and should depart, like other institutions such as the county regiment, into the halls of hallowed memory, and, if so, we should go without complaint.[57]

Many Free Church leaders, however, were planning to depart ecumenically. But there were obstacles. Baptists, Congregationalists and Methodists in Wales failed to conclude ecumenical negotiations with the Anglican Church of Wales, partly because none of the Churches involved could really decide whether union within the Principality might prejudice more attractive opportunities for ecumenism on a larger stage. After long formal conversations, the Church of England and the Methodist Church failed, a decade ago, to achieve union, although Methodism, the weaker of the two prospective partners, actually endorsed the terms negotiated. Anglican reservations – including hopes of alternative, and grander, mergers – proved too strong for the union to be consummated. But in 1972 the first ecumenical enterprise to transcend denominational boundaries was achieved: the Congregational Church of England and Wales and the Presbyterian Church of England desappeared into a new United Reformed Church.

While particular failures are reminders of the complexity, conflict and compromise involved in sacrificing historic religious traditions, even in the interests of survival, they also provide evidence of a continuing ecumenical preoccupation in British Christianity. Indeed, the 'decisive difference' between Christian life in Britain in the nineteenth and twentieth centuries has been the substitution of a co-operative spirit for a competitive one.[58] Moreover the change has been evident not just at the level of formal ecumenical 'conversations', but even more, perhaps, in attitudes and activities typical of local, regional and often *ad hoc* Christian enterprises. Joint-services, co-operative evangelism and resource-sharing at a local level have increased greatly; membership transfers have reached a point where it is evident that lay people in many cases have little commitment to the distinctive features of particular denominations;[59] and the siting of new churches often has become a co-operative exercise concerned neither to duplicate nor threaten the existing activities of other denominations.

The British Council of Churches, established in 1942, has spawned hundreds of constituent local Councils of Churches, and considerable progress towards Christian unity has been made at a succession of twentieth-century ecumenical conferences held mainly in England. The 'Faith and Order' and 'Life and Work' conferences of the 1920s and 1930s, the Nottingham 'Faith and Order' Conference of 1964 and the Birmingham Church Leaders' Conference of 1972 (with its historic development, the presence of Catholic representatives), have given a certain substance to the dream of a British Christianity united in the face of secularization, despite the relative failure of moves towards organic union.

The last of these conferences, bringing church leaders together in the Selly Oak Colleges, Birmingham, in September 1972, left no doubt about the context in which ecumenism makes its appeal. In an elaboration of 'The Reasons for the Conference', the man who had first conceived the idea of holding it, David L. Edwards, remarked bluntly: 'The Conference was unprecedented, for the crisis it faced is without precedent.' He went on to point out that not only were recent statistics of declining church attendances, membership and finance 'alarming', but that 'most thoughtful observers expect worse statistics to come.' Young people, especially, seemed more than ever alienated from the Churches, and Edwards was merely echoing a general apprehension in predicting that, 'The alienation of this new generation will, if unchecked, bring greater and greater disasters as the Church's ageing leadership and membership dies . . .'.[60]

Interestingly, in one of the finest speeches at the Conference, Cardinal John Heenan, Catholic Archbishop of Westminster, struck a jarring note even as he predicted the eventual success of ecumenism. Unity was inevitable, he implied, because secularization seemed bound to continue. But what kind of unity? 'In God's good time', said the Archbishop,

we shall talk not of the churches but of one church. This, at least, seems certain – Christians will never return to the old rivalries and enmities. As religious belief declines in the West they will unite in an evangelical spirit to preach Christ to their brethren and lead them to the One Holy Catholic and Apostolic Church.[61]

But this was not, of course, the kind of ecumenism which most of the assembled church leaders had in mind. It was not the Cardinal's proud Catholicism which alarmed them, but his uncompromising attitude towards the secular world. Prior to the concluding statement just quoted, his tone had been stern and didactic. He had rejected totally the idea of a Church re-united on the basis of compromise with the beliefs and values of the post-Christian age, and he feared a softening or abandonment of traditional doctrines designed to make the historic gospel more acceptable to secular men. 'Although for ecumenical reasons the word heretic is not used today', he had remarked pointedly, 'heretics still exist. The chief heresy is what we used to call modernism.'[62]

As the Cardinal sat down one Catholic priest in the audience, embarrassed by the 'unhappy reactions' around him, 'had to be carried off to the bar by two of his friends – both Anglican bishops – and fortified with large whiskies until he had recovered'. The Cardinal, however, had faced the really basic issue. Was the majority of British Christian leaders and lay people right in the belief that the modern Church had to *accommodate* itself to the modern world, or was the opposing minority right in insisting that *resistance* was the only genuinely Christian response to secularization? 'This', remarked Edwards, 'remained a question for which large whiskies could find no answer.'[63] For if the danger of accommodation was reduction to spiritual nothingness, the inescapable implication of resistance was that, after 1,500 years, Christianity as a whole was slipping once more into its primitive role as a sect – as a sub-culture at odds with its contemporary world.

# NOTES

1. Berger, P. (1961), p. 41.
2. *Wesleyan Conference Minutes*, 1900, p. 404.
3. Dale, A. W. W. (1902), p. 312.
4. *Wesleyan Conference Minutes*, 1898, p. 423.
5. *Contemporary Review*, XXXI (March 1878), p. 708.
6. *Chronicles of Convocation*, 1974, pp. 63-4.
7. The Harris Poll, 'The Religious Beliefs of the British People' (Report on a Survey Carried out from 13-19 April, 1970), p. 5.
8. Independent Television Authority (1970), p. 19.
9. Edwards, D. L. (1973), p. 81.
10. Mudie-Smith, R. (1904), pp. 43-4, 307-13.
11. Ibid.
12. Smith, B. J. (1898), p. 6.
13. Ibid.
14. The figures are from the denomination's official annual handbook, *Y Blwyddiadur, neu, Lyfr swyddogol y Methodistiaid Calfinaidd*.
15. *Catholic Times*, 7 June 1957; *Daily Express*, 30 May 1957.
16. Pickering, W. S. F. (1968), p. 83.
17. *Chronicles of Convocation*, 1901, p. 150.
18. Chadwick, O. (1970), p. 168.
19. Soloway, R. A. (1969), p. 11.
20. Chadwick, O. (1970), p. 170.
21. *Chronicles of Convocation*, 1901, p. 146.
22. *Contemporary Review*, LXXXIX (March 1906), p. 716.
23. Paul, L. (1964), p. 112.
24. Ibid., p. 136.
25. *Church Times*, 28 January 1977.
26. Ibid., 4 February 1977.
27. Gilmore, A. (ed.) (1971), p. 4.
28. Ibid., p. 54.
29. Carlton, E. (1968), p. 112.
30. Gilmore, A. (ed.) (1971), p. 35.
31. Davidson, N. (1965), p. 9.
32. Gilmore, A. (ed.) (1971), pp. 35, 47.
33. *The Times*, 11 February 1967.
34. Edwards, D. L. (1973), p. 39.
35. Gilmore, A. (ed.) (1971), p. 46.
36. Ibid.
37. Towler, R. (1969), pp. 112-15.
38. Ibid., p. 115.
39. *Chronicles of Convocation*, 1974, p. 29.
40. *Congregational Year Book*, 1939, p. 75.
41. Berger, P. (1969), p. 158.
42. Bonhoeffer, D. (1953), pp. 122-3.
43. Nicholls, W. (1969), p. 233.
44. Edwards, D. L. (1963), p. 7.
45. Rowntree, B. S. and Lavers, B. R. (1951), p. 50.
46. Edwards, D. L. (1963), pp. 49, 50.

47. Ibid., pp. 92-3.
48. Ibid., p. 215.
49. Ibid., pp. 222–3.
50. Quoted by Martin, D. (1979), p. 16.
51. Ibid., p. 15.
52. Ibid., p. 16.
53. *Anglican-Methodist Unity, Part 2: The Scheme* (SPCK and Epworth, London, 1968), p. 7.
54. Gilbert, A. D. (1976), pp. 58-9.
55. Currie, R. (1968), p. 316.
56. Ibid., p. 314.
57. *British Weekly*, 22 October 1959, p. 11.
58. Davies, H. (1965), p. 5.
59. See, for example, the data in Currie, R., Gilbert, A. D. and Horsley, L. H. (1977), pp. 184–8.
60. Edwards, D. L. (1973), pp. 2-3.
61. Ibid., p. 29.
62. Ibid.
63. Ibid., p. 30.

CHAPTER SIX

# Limits to secularization

If ecumenism reflects the growing convergence of diverse Christian traditions which secularization has stripped of ancient theological certainties and historic denominational peculiarities, it is noteworthy that a minority of British Christians is vehemently anti-ecumenical. Accommodation is not the only possible response to the emergence of a post-Christian culture. But in the last resort there is but one alternative: the lonely sectarian road of resistance. Secularization, in short, is beginning to polarize Christians into camps so far apart, so dissimilar, that in the future all other alignments and differences may become not just secondary, but irrelevant. The American theologian, John B. Cobb, put it clearly in an observation during the 'Honest to God' debate of the 1960s:

We may really take the modern world seriously, acknowledge that it is the only world we know, accept it, affirm it, and live it. To do so is to accept and live the death of God. On the other hand, we may refuse the modern world, distance ourselves from it, fence in our world of traditional faith, and seek to preserve it from the corrosion of the world outside. Both expedients are desperate ones.[1]

And precisely because both expedients are desperate, neither gets much explicit acknowledgement, or even, apparently, much conscious recognition as a basis for relationships between the 'Church' and the 'world'. Christians advocating the accommodation of Christian beliefs and values to modern secular consciousness do not, for they cannot, accept that in the process the religious culture will itself be thoroughly secularized, or that the essence of Christianity will be dissipated. Synthesis is the aim, even when the result gets perilously close to capitulation. By the same logic, the strategy of resistance co-exists with the hope that by refusal to compromise Christianity will increase, not relinquish, its capacity for influencing the 'world'. Attempts to 'fence

133

in' the traditional faith, to reject 'worldliness', can be sustained by the optimistic assumption that withdrawal will not mean cultural marginality and irrelevance – that a post-Christian culture does, in fact, 'hunger and thirst' after genuine, uncompromising righteousness.

But heads buried, ostrich fashion, are not likely to make reliable strategic decisions. Outside observers often see more clearly. Alastair MacIntyre, we have noted, saw Bishop Robinson as an atheist. David Boulton, in the socialist review *Tribune*, was equally uncompromising. 'God', he said,

once meant something clear and definite. So did 'heaven' and 'prayer' and 'worship'. Was there any point in my continuing to use the same words but giving each of them a special, private meaning? Was this not to invite misunderstanding? To say 'God' instead of talking about 'the depth and ground of history' was certainly to save breath, but did not the word 'God' have so many unwelcome associations that the longer word was actually preferable?[2]

Attempts to be 'honest-to-god', Boulton confessed, 'made me cease to apply to myself the label "Christian"'. It is evident where his sympathies would have rested at the Church Leaders' Conference discussed at the end of our previous chapter. A few months prior to the conference a young British theologian, Alastair Kee, in *The Way of Transcendence*,[3] had argued that to survive Christianity would have to jettison its belief in God. This was a candid statement of the accommodatory thinking which the uncompromising Catholic, Cardinal Heenan, branded as 'heresy' – much to the distress of liberal-minded conferees. Yet it is evident that the question of whether or not Kee's position is 'heretical' simply must be faced if the Christian Churches are to make any stand against secularization. Tolerance, obfuscation and theological ambivalence are unlikely to survive indefinitely the polarization of Christian attitudes to the modern world, and polarization seems inevitable.

For accommodation is reaching critical limits. It is hard to avoid the conclusion that the response of liberal Protestantism to the modernization of Western culture points towards its ultimate extinction as a religious culture. Maybe it is not actually dying. 'Metamorphosis' may provide a more precise metaphor than the ideas of 'death' or 'suicide' to describe this theologian-led march from traditional Protestantism to Protestant secularity. Protestant associations may not vanish – they may simply cease to be, in any meaningful way, 'religious'. But, either way, to answer Paul van Buren's famous question, 'How may a Christian who is himself a secular man understand the Gospel?' may be simpler than his 200 pages of analysis would suggest. A truly secular man cannot understand it.

He can call himself 'Christian' only by destroying the traditional meaning of the term.

What then is likely to be the future of religion in a post-Christian Britain? If it cannot accommodate itself to the modern culture must it, to survive, resist that culture? Must it accept the realities of becoming sub-cultural? Must it, in short, return to its primitive role as a sectarian movement in a pagan world, and bear the inescapable losses of power, status, respectability and social influence which such a change implies? As Berger has remarked, 'The sect, in its classical sociology-of-religion conception, serves as the model for organizing a cognitive minority *against* a hostile or at least non-believing milieu'.[4] Thus if and when a Church accepts that its environment really has become post-Christian, the radical course of thorough-going sectarianism may indeed be the best way to maximise its residual cultural influence.

Obviously, such a strategy would make sense over the long term only if there are definite limits to secularization. If there are no such limits, the resistance of a sectarian sub-culture can be only temporary, for the secularization of consciousness and behaviour eventually will prove irresistible. The sect will go the way of the denomination, only with less dignity. But there are various grounds upon which it is possible to argue that the impact of secularization, although powerful and pervasive, is subject to certain limits. Some, particularly those based on theological premises, are unlikely to convince anyone outside the confines of sectarian conviction; others should be taken seriously by uncommitted social scientists and sociologists.

In the first place, once the costly sectarian commitment has been made a Christian sub-culture acquires an ideological orientation permitting it to exploit various kinds of discontent within the wider secular (and indeed denominational) environment. Unless the social, cultural and psychological conditions of modern life eventually reach utopian levels of perfection, for all individuals and classes, there will remain reservoirs of people feeling deprived, dissatisfied or disillusioned within the 'modern' world. Some of them will have absolutely no predeliction towards any kind of religion, and a small, eccentric sub-culture presumably will have no obvious appeal to anything but a minority of them. What they will represent, however, will be a limited constituency which is insulated, at least partially, from the dominant assumptions and values through which secularization has been mediated and sustained.

In Britain, since the Second World War while evidence of secularization has increased rapidly both in the mainstream society and the life of the major Churches, modern sect of various kinds have succeeded in exploiting such constituencies. The following figures relate to Mormon and Seventh-Day Adventist 'members' and Jehovah's Witnesses' 'publishers' (an equivalent category), between 1940 and 1970:[5]

|      | Mormons | Jehovah's Witnesses | Seventh-Day Adventists |
|------|---------|---------------------|------------------------|
| 1940 | 6,364   | 8,823               | 5,915                  |
| 1950 | 6,357   | 20,936              | 6,666                  |
| 1960 | 17,332  | 43,650              | 9,277                  |
| 1970 | 68,217  | 59,705              | 12,145                 |

In the 1970s, annual figures indicate a deceleration of these growth processes, a development which probably reflects both the limits of the sectarian constituency and the incorrigible tendency for numerical growth to sap the earlier vitality of a sect. Sheer size brings a measure of respectability and social acceptance, which in turn introduce the problems of worldliness and compromise which, as sociologists explained long ago, set a sect on the road towards denominationalism.

In the context of the present argument, however, what the figures show is the capacity of at least some forms of sectarian religion to exploit the very social circumstances in which denominational religion declines. Some sects are more 'conversionist' than others; some are almost totally uninterested in augmenting their numbers. Only in the early 1950s, for example, did a change of leadership in the Mormon Church produce a renewed, intense commitment to evangelization.[6] But the fact remains that a conversionist sect can achieve *progressive* growth at a time when secularization has condemned the denominations to *recessive*, even *residual* growth patterns. The secret lies in the difference between the sectarian and the denominational constituency.

While the denomination seeks to assure the secular mind that religion, too, can be secular, the sect speaks to people who, for whatever reason, find their consciousness at odds with the dominant culture. Thus the denomination appeals to a very wide constituency, but with very little hope of turning many constituents into church members; whereas the sect appeals to a highly restricted constituency, but with a distinctiveness of goals and an intensity of commitment which enables it to mobilize its constituents towards membership. For ideological reasons, moreover, the sect can adjust to the indifference or hostility of a secular environment better than the denomination can. Decline can produce demoralization in the latter, first in the professional ministry and then also among the laity. But in a sect, being a tiny, despised minority can be seen merely to confirm the typically sectarian 'remnant theology'. The Pauline question, 'When the Son of Man cometh shall He find faith in the earth?' might hold alarming implications for a denominational Christian who took it literally, yet in many sectarian circles it is a favourite text, for it smacks of reality and challenges the remnant to endure.

The second, deeper level at which the sectarian strategy of resistance to secularization is likely to survive in a post-Christian society, is the level at which no foreseeable developments in the modernization process can reach the roots of human religiosity. One thing Christianity shares with secularization, ironically, is that 'the last enemy is death'! For while all people continue to die, some people will continue to be religious. The impact of this final 'breaking point' certainly has been blunted by the cultural context of secular humanism and the social realities of advanced medicine and institutionalized care of the aged and terminally ill. But like sexuality in Victorian bourgeois consciousness, it will not go away; it is an enduring, if somewhat incongruous, aspect of human existence in the modern world. And as the unvanquished guardian of human spirituality, it sets apparently inviolable limits to the advance of secularization.

Moreover, the finitude of human life is not the only restriction on the emergence and maintenance of thoroughly 'secular' consciousness. *Any* reminder of the powerlessness of humankind or the contingent nature of human achievement breaks the illusion of 'the autonomy of man and the world', and in so doing can prompt 'religious' questions and responses. The dazzling effects of modernization may have pushed all the 'breaking-points' into the periphery of the taken-for-granted world of modern man, and so long as modern industrial society endures secularization is likely to hold them there. But their very existence will continue to release a subterranean spirituality into modern, post-Christian consciousness, and (more significantly for the present argument) the minority of the population which does directly confront them will continue to provide a constituency for the traditional, other-worldly religion which the sects represent.

## PATTERNS OF RESISTANCE

With varying degrees of reluctance and hesitation, certain elements within all the mainstream British Churches have turned, or are

137

beginning to turn, away from accommodation and towards the
sectarian alternative of resistance to secularization. The tendency has
been much more prevalent in some denominations and Churches than
in others. By far the most important vertical division has been that
separating Catholics and Protestants, for although ambivalent on
certain issues, British Catholicism generally has stood firm against the
temptation to compromise with the emerging post-Christian culture.
But the division is not essentially related to *any* ancient ecclesiastical
difference. Within mainstream Protestantism, for example, the
Baptists, as a denomination, have been distinguished by an uncompromising attitude comparable in its tenacity with the Catholic
resistance, and all the denominations still contain minority movements
with the same characteristics.

Negative responses to secularization thus have a religious–cultural
basis which transcends denominational divisions. Indeed resistance
produces its own distinctive brand of ecumenism or (more precisely) of
anti-ecumenism. For paralleling the ecumenity of the British and World
Councils of Churches, and the conventional denominational
ecumenism of mainstream British Protestantism, there exists a kind of
'shadow ecumenism', its unity arising partly from a shared rejection of
precisely those ideological compromises which have facilitated the
'official' ecumenical movement by eroding traditional differences
between Christians.

This distinction would not, of course, be acceptable to the
mainstream ecumenical leadership. The 'official' line would echo the
views which Albert van den Heuvel, a leader in the World Council of
Churches, popularized in the 1960s in his influential study, *The
Humiliation of the Church*. He argued that ecumenicity embraces many
ecclesiastical and spiritual tendencies, some of them in considerable
tension with certain others. Distinguishing, in particular, between
*individual, churchly* and *secular* modes of ecumenism, he saw each as a
part of an emerging whole, mutually enriching the work of the
'Church' in the 'world'. But his analysis became uneasy, to say the least,
in exploring actual differences between these modes. *Personal*
ecumenism, he acknowledged, arose from the sharing of a common
evangelical pietism; but *churchly* and *secular* ecumenism, on the other
hand, were preoccupied with 'the reunification of the historic
confessions rather than the personal enrichment of the participants.' Far
from enriching a traditional form of personal pietism, the latter saw the
way forward as something requiring 'the rediscovery of the world'
through a 'new and positive evaluation of secularization.' There could
scarcely be a clearer manifestation of the distinction between

accommodation and resistance.[7]

Ecumenicists, for obvious reasons of ideology and temperament, often become blind to fundamental contradictions. Personal, pietistical 'experiments in unity and renewal' were gratefully acknowledged by van den Heuval when they took the form of the YMCA, the YWCA, or similar, essentially secularized movements, but they were charged with 'sentimentality and emotionalism, naiveté and otherworldliness', when they took the form of the Evangelical Alliance, a powerful expression of what is here described as 'shadow ecumenism'.[8] For the Alliance was not the kind of *personal* ecumenism with which *churchly* and *secular* ecumenists could enter meaningful relationships. Rather, to them it exemplified certain 'dangers' inherent in personal ecumenism: the 'danger' of assuming 'that the basic reality in life is the soul's personal relation to God', the 'danger' of exclusiveness – of uniting only with 'those to whom we feel akin', and the 'danger' of rejecting the wider culture.[9] But such an analysis simply falsifies reality. In modern British Christianity the Evangelical Alliance is not an extreme, isolated aberration within what van den Heuval calls *personal* ecumenism, it is the outstanding example of the phenomenon. What he calls the 'dangers' of the position are in fact its defining characteristics!

Ironically, in 1966, the year *The Humiliation of the Church* was published, the Evangelical Alliance promoted a National Assembly of Evangelicals, and through it was responsible for establishing a Commission on Evangelism entrusted with the task of studying ways and means to 'promote a new emphasis on personal evangelism' in Britain. The Commission's report, entitled, significantly, *On the Other Side*, showed just how naive was the idea that co-operative ventures based on evangelical individualism could ever be regarded simply as troublesome elements in a wider ecumenical movement. Such ventures, the report explained, grew out of a genuine Christian opposition to secularization, and to the fashionable ecumenism which had surrendered to the secular *zeitgeist*. No fellowship between the two was possible. The *churchly* and *secular* ecumenists seemed to be travelling on that broad road of which Christ had spoken so chillingly. 'In the last analysis', *On the Other Side* asserted,

there is only one distinction to be made; that is, between those who believe in the essentials of the Gospel and those who do not. This fundamental distinction is drawn sharply in the New Testament, as sharply as the difference between darkness and light, death and life.[10]

Co-operation was 'impossible', these evangelicals concluded, with liberal 'Christians' who 'falsify the Gospel by subtracting from it'. Like Cardinal Heenan in the speech quoted earlier, they viewed accommodation as a modern heresy. Rather than 'producing a theology for the secular world', *secular* ecumenists 'produce a secularized theology, devoid of any supernatural elements and sometimes detached from its historic basis as well'.[11]

It is precisely such uncompromising attitudes and language which make an accommodation-resistance distinction fundamental to understanding modern relationships between the 'Church' and the 'world'. The lines are already firmly drawn, even if many individuals and institutions remain, divided or uncertain, on some middle ground. But the shaping of an alternative, essentially sectarian religious culture, has advanced in parallel to the progress of secular ecumenism. Neither movement has yet come fully to fruition, but both seem certain to dictate future patterns of British Christianity. Paralleling the successes of official ecumenism in the 1960s and 1970s, for example, the 'shadow ecumenism' has gained strength from the renewed vitality of the Evangelical Alliance, the calling of the National Evangelical Assembly, the emergence of the Inter-Varsity Fellowship as a body influential far beyond its size, and the appearance of new, inter-denominational groupings of 'Evangelical Free Churches'. The negative response to secularization inherent in each of these developments makes them symptoms of the widening horizontal division in British Christianity between, on the one hand, liberal strategies of accommodation and, on the other, conservative strategies of resistance.

But if evangelical orthodoxy now seems unchallenged for the leadership of Protestant resistance to secularization, its hegemony has been established fairly recently. Historically, negative responses to modernization in both religion and society have also arisen in quite different religious cultural milieux. At least since the 1830s, for example, High Church Anglicanism has maintained a nostalgic, anti-industrial, anti-modern animus hostile to most cultural manifestations of secularization, and from the 1880s to the eve of the Second World War it was implicated deeply in intellectual and social activities concerned to reverse or humanize modern cultural trends.[12] Notwithstanding such involvements, however, there has always been something too dilettantish about Anglo-Catholicism for it to mobilize and sustain a popular religious reaction.

But Pentecostalism did, for a time, seem well-suited for such a role. Much more dynamic, just a decade or so ago, than it appears today, it represented, to some observers, a 'Fourth Force' potentially capable of arresting the decline of Christianity in the West. It was able both to attract people indifferent to mainstream denominationalism, and to infuse elements within almost every denominational community with a spiritualism capable of transcending established eccesiastical loyalties. Indifference to institutionalized loyalties was at once a negative and a creative force. Church leaders and denominational assemblies feared the threat of entire local congregations going over to Pentecostalist activities and concerns, and in the process losing respect for traditional authority-structures, liturgy and evangelism. But Pentecostalism could also promote its own particular brand of 'shadow ecumenism'.

The essential Pentecostalist concerns – with the gifts of the Spirit in the lives of 'born again' believers, including the gifts of tongues and healing; and with the possibility of re-living, in the contemporary age, that first Pentecost when the Holy Ghost filled the apostolic Church with power, hope, faith and joy – these things exercised a commanding fascination for many modern Christians confronted by a world indifferent and a Church demoralized. Catholic priests and laity, Anglican clergy and sometimes entire Church of England congregations, and significant elements within all other Churches were oddly at one in an over-riding desire to experience the 'fullness of the Spirit'. Sometimes they held joint-services, and they seemed commonly to adopt an impatient, almost condenscending attitude to the less-profusive, traditional spirituality of denominational brethren.

Conflict between mainstream denominationalism and Pentecostalism went deeper than differences of style and intensity, however. Basically it was a difference about attitudes to the secularization of the Church. For Pentecostalism provided theological and experiential re-assurance for Christians opposed to compromise with the secular 'world'. If an empiricist rationality was undermining the plausibility of historic revelation as an objective basis of faith, a new subjectivism promised to free Christianity from the corrosive influences of modernization. It was, in short, a religious equivalent of those varieties of secular mysticism which, in the 1960s particularly, attracted a young generation bent on 'dropping out' of modern technological society. For Christians concerned to resist worldly attitudes, beliefs and values, it was, in the words of the Catholic scholar, E. I. Watkin, a 'withdrawal, enforced by the progress of science and historical research, to a theology of spiritual experience . . .'.[13]

This was a thoroughly sectarian orientation to the wider society. Pentecostalists, especially within one of the discrete Pentecostal sects like the Elim Foursquare Gospel Alliance, but also when they retained denominational associations, formed a 'cognitive minority' consciously at odds with a 'hostile', faithless culture. They were marginal in a sense in which even orthodox evangelicals, for all their theological conservatism, were not. And this has been a disadvantage as the crisis of contemporary Christianity has deepened. The bulk of Pentecostalists might be evangelical in their understanding of God, Sin, Salvation, Incarnation and Atonement, but the majority of evangelicals evidently feel uneasy about an understanding of Christian spirituality likely to alienate potential converts on non-essential grounds. Evangelicalism is a conversionist movement. Rejecting the secular culture, it still wants to convert secular men and women. Its resistance, in short, is – at least in theory – an aggressive posture; and in the crisis, when exponents of traditional orthodoxy are concerned to maximize the forces of resistance, Pentecostalism has seemed a somewhat self-indulgent luxury that the minority cannot afford. Its influence has receded accordingly during the past decade or so.

If resistance is to be the strategy of Christian survival, then, the prophetic role almost certainly belongs – in the case of British Protestantism, at least – to the forces of evangelical orthodoxy. Evangelicalism is increasingly well-organized at an inter-denominational and undenominational level, as the authority of the Evangelical Alliance indicates, but its resources are still deployed chiefly within denominational structures. How long existing denominational patterns will endure may depend on the speed with which ecumenical developments bring to a head tensions between liberal and conservative interests. In the meantime, however, examining the strength of evangelicalism involves a denomination-by-denomination survey.

## Anglicanism

The Church of England, linked constitutionally with the temporal authority of the State, has always tended, however reluctantly, to come to terms with changes in its cultural environment. Emerging from a sixteenth-century accommodation between Church and State, its history has seen mainstream Anglicanism sometimes as a vehicle of cultural change, sometimes as a kind of national conscience, but never, for long, in a sectarian relationship with its English 'world'. Yet within the Church powerful currents have from time to time taken resistance to external cultural developments, including secularization, to the point of virtual sectarianism. The Oxford Movement is an obvious example. It was 'before all else anti-liberal',[14] and its young leaders spurned, with a special intensity, the utilitarian accommodation between the ecclesiastical pragmatism of Bishop Blomfield and the liberal-toryism of Sir Robert Peel. Ultimately, of course, their commitment to resistance took the most adamant of them outside the Church, into a nineteenth-century Catholicism where uncompromising conservatism was possible.

Anglican evangelicalism has never entered so extreme and hostile a relationship with its host religious culture. Indeed, at various times – notably during the mid-Victorian era – it has come close to dominating Anglicanism, and through it English society at large. Its Victorian apogee was short-lived, however. Its dogmatic, other-worldly theology was more manifestly at odds with the growing secularity of late-Victorian culture than were other strands of Anglican churchmanship; and by the late nineteenth century evangelicalism was declining as an influence in Church and society alike, even if its residual moral authority and its carefully-guarded parochial strongholds survived to mask for many years the full extent of its decline. As late as 1970 the evangelicals were still sufficiently strong in ecclesiastical party terms to exercise a decisive influence against Anglican-Methodist union, but it had become clear, nevertheless, that the instinctive mainstream tendency towards accommodation had turned them, on most issues, into a sect within a liberal denominational culture.

If accommodation has been an instinctive reaction for many Anglicans, the instinct has, in some cases, been reinforced by an acute awareness of the alternatives. As early as 1936, for example, contributing to a symposium on *The Church and the Twentieth Century*, a non-evangelical Bishop of Birmingham, Ernest W. Barnes, recognized that secularization, with its 'new *zeitgeist*' of rationalistic humanism, had left Anglicanism facing the polar alternatives of adaptation or (as he put it explicitly) decline into sectarianism. Twentieth-century Britain had become, in its 'almost unconscious activity of mind and spirit', a secular society. 'The historic churches – the Church of England included – must', the Bishop argued, either 'adapt themselves to this *zeitgeist* or become sectarian minorities, struggling, highly organized, probably waspish . . .'.[15] Like the Bishop of Woolwich twenty-seven years later, Barnes accepted the full implications of such adaptation. 'Much that our fathers believed must perish,' he said. 'Let it perish'. He was content to believe that 'an empirically reached theism will ultimately maintain itself ', along with an appropriate Christian ethic.[16] Evangelicals, however, have simply refused to countenance such compromises. So far they have been content to fight secularizing tendencies from within the Church – a sect legitimated by its liberal, respectable denominational environment. The future, however, may press the question of just how far ecclesiastical and theological compromise can go before this relationship becomes untenable.

The differences certainly are immense. Robert Towler, whose

analysis of the beliefs, values and behaviour of different types of Anglican ordinands has been discussed earlier, has recognized the relevance of the classical 'church'-'sect' distinction to his discovery of profound differences between *puritan* and *antipuritan* types of ministerial candidates. The puritans, essentially evangelical in theology, have a 'strong sense of the supernatural', attach great importance to 'religious and other-worldly values at the expense of this-worldly values', and display 'withdrawal from the world and aversion to the cultural values of secular society'.[17] Their position, like that of the evangelical laity from which they come, is at once aggressively evangelistic and, to quote Bryan Wilson's definition of conversionist sectarianism, as Towler has, 'distrustful of, or indifferent towards, the denominations and churches which have at best diluted, at worst betrayed, Christianity . . .'.[18]

This is an arresting analysis, for it reinforces other evidence suggesting that the primary loyalties of the evangelicals lie, not so much with the Anglican tradition *per se*, as with the religious-cultural alignment of evangelicalism generally against secularization and liberal Protestantism. Consequently, it is not difficult to conceive of evangelical Anglicans abandoning their historic denominational position more or less *en masse* in the event of any major ecumenical rationalisation of mainstream Christianity in Britain. Even now, although evidently reluctant to precipitate a crisis involving ecclesiastical re-alignments, they tend to find religious satisfactions and responsibilities either exclusively within a local evangelical parish community, or beyond it in non-denominational environments like the Evangelical Alliance, the Inter-Varsity Fellowship or the Keswick Convention.

## Presbyterianism.

British Presbyterianism is a heterogeneous religious culture, with Scottish, Irish and Welsh Presbyterians representing a variety of theological, regional and social orientations. Welsh Presbyterians, for example, have in many respects always been closer to the English Dissenters than to either Scottish or Irish Presbyterians. Comparable patterns of synodical polity and a common acceptance of Calvinist principles do, however, give some substance to the common denominational label. And as far as the impact of secularization has been concerned, an important common feature has been the relative isolation of areas of Presbyterian strength from that metropolitan English culture to which the term 'post-Christian' is most evidently applicable.

As a result the kind of analytical framework implied by the accommodation-resistance distinction, while not unilluminating, is somewhat premature in the context of Presbyterian religion. The modern crisis in relationships between 'Church' and 'world' has developed less acutely for the Presbyterian Churches, certainly at a cultural level, and the tensions between strategies of accommodation and resistance remain correspondingly under-developed.

There are remote Welsh villages and isolated fishing hamlets in Scotland's Western Isles where neither the life of kirk or chapel, nor the taken-for-granted acceptance of religion as a vital aspect of normal existence, has changed much in the past couple of centuries. Secularization – along with modernization in most of its manifestations – has passed such places by. But while these are unusual situations, there is a sense in which the impact of secularization has been delayed, in most non-English areas of the British Isles, by an understandable Celtic reaction against English cultural imperialism. 'Celtic fringe' may be an offensive phrase, but, stripped of any derogatory overtones, it describes an important reality. 'Compared with the situation in Britain and Europe,' an official Presbyterian Church in Ireland publication proclaimed in 1971, referring specifically to Ulster, 'ours are a Church-going people'. But it went on to warn against complacency. To preserve its unusually high level of religiosity, the Church acknowledged, Ulster would have to resist 'ideas and influences from overseas'.[19] This was a tacit admission that the strength of Irish Presbyterianism arose, in part, from its cultural isolation.

In fact, the social environment of the Presbyterian Church in Ireland combines with its powerful evangelicalism to create a patently sectarian orientation to the modern 'world'. Sect-like, it remains suspicious about secular entertainments such as gambling, it is opposed to the legalization of Sunday sport, cinema and theatre, it campaigns fiercely for tighter censorship of 'lewd and pornographic' publications, it favours temperance, fears secular education, and castigates liberal attitudes, believing they can only produce 'counterfeit Christians' and create a vacuous Christianity in which 'worldliness masquerades under the cloak of piety'.[20] On ecumenism, too, while the familiar horizontal division between liberals and conservatives is reproduced in Ulster, the liberal ecumenists are in a minority. The majority inclination is sternly against compromise. In the conflict between conservatives and ecumenists, the 1971 Report explained, 'the vast majority of Christians know that to abandon the historic roots of Christianity is to abandon reality'.[21]

In Scotland Presbyterianism is the Established religion, and to the status and prestige of its official position is added a popular influence much stronger than that which Anglicanism has managed to maintain in England. The sectarian strategy of resistance naturally assumes no pressing urgency in such circumstances, partly because the decline of religion has not reached the point where accommodation means virtual de-christianization by compromise. In England, for example, after the 'Honest to God' debate the division between liberal and conservative attitudes to the secular world went much deeper than the simple question of whether or not old truths could, or should, be expressed in new ways. Accommodation, Robinson insisted, meant 'far more than a restating of traditional orthodoxy in modern terms'.[22] But for most of Scottish Presbyterianism's leading theologians it still meant precisely such a restatement. It was a question, wrote the minister of Glagow's Cathedral Church in 1965, of Christianity 'getting its Gospel across to the man-in-the-street who is often reluctant to listen.' The quest for wider social authority and influence still seemed realistic, and there was no evident contradiction in demanding both that the Church should be 'loyal to "the faith once delivered to the saints" ', and that it should be 'at the same time sensitive to the spirit of the age'.[23]

Secularization, in short, had not proceeded far enough to drive the inevitable wedge between these twin goals of worldly influence and spiritual integrity. But already there were hints that, if and when the hard choices imposed on the 'Church' in a post-Christian 'world' became inescapable for Scottish Presbyterians, ancient traditions of stern calvinistic orthodoxy would produce a strong, possibly majority decision, in favour of resistance. Nevile Davidson, his secular prestige as Chaplain to the Queen in Scotland notwithstanding, foreshadowed as much over a decade ago when he warned that,

The Church, if it is to exert its proper influence and make its unique contribution to the life of the nation and the world, must be the Church. Not a voluntary society with a kindly humanitarian outlook and an idealistic philosophy, not a powerful organization, making its impact upon society by its able leaders, its efficient methods of recruitment, its streamlined structure of administration, its valuable 'contacts', its venerable history and traditions. If we rely on such things . . . then the acids of secularism will inevitably poison the life of the Christian community, and sap its spiritual strength.[24]

## The Free Churches

Until the closing decades of the nineteenth century the English Free Churches – the Nonconformists, as they were more commonly known until the present century – remained, like their Scottish, Welsh and Irish counterparts, almost uniformly evangelical. But a decline of Free Church evangelicalism accompanied the growing respectability of the chapel, and the gradual integration of chapel folk into the mainstream of English society. Older sectarian tendencies inherited from the era when social opprobrium and civil disabilities had been part and parcel of Nonconformist commitment, gave way to denominational characteristics, among them a new tolerance of alternative social and religious conventions and a growing desire to come to terms with wider theological and intellectual cultures. Laymen wealthier and socially more assured, ministers now linked in fraternal associations with Anglican clergymen, chapel communities becoming merely one of several associational involvements for many of their members – such things left the Free Churches open to all the pressures favouring compromise with the secular culture. The result has been the emergence of a theological and emotional dichotomy comparable with that imposed by secularization of modern Anglicanism, and (outside the Baptist denomination), majority opinion has followed the mainstream Anglican pattern of progressive accommodation.

In Congregationalism, as Chapter Five has noted, the search for a 'preachable' gospel involved various early departures from evangelical orthodoxy, and as early as the 1890s the pioneer sociologist, Charles Booth, was convinced that a majority of the denomination was moving 'towards unorthodoxy'. There was a tendency, he discovered, for Congregational lay people to regard faith in Christ 'not primarily as that which involves faith in the great sacrifice of a risen saviour, but rather as the acceptance of an ideal affecting human life and human relationships which may be described as "Christian humanitarianism"'.[25] Booth would not have been surprised by the appearance of Campbell's 'New Theology' in 1907, nor perhaps by what a reviewer had to say about Nathaniel Micklem's *What is Faith?*, which appeared in 1936. Micklem's aim was to re-assert traditional orthodoxy in Congregationalism, and unless he was wrong, Douglas Landridge told readers of the *Congregational Quarterly*, 'half our ministers are preaching, and half our laymen are believing, a mere parody of Christianity'.[26]

With scholars like H. F. Lovell Cocks, Daniel Jenkins and John Marsh, Micklem was at the centre of a conservative reaction to the bland liberalism of the 1920s. They published widely, and after setting up *The Presbyter* as a vehicle for their views in 1942, established a Church Order Group in 1946 to give further coherence to their position. Without adopting uncompromising resistance to modern liberal tendencies, this kind of initiative certainly slowed down the secularization of Congregational theology in the 1940s and 1950s. It nurtured a threatened orthodoxy, albeit without really insulating the denomination from 'modern' influences, and by so doing preserved a place in Congregationalism for what was, by the mid-twentieth century, a minority evangelicalism. The possibility that some Congregationalists might feel drawn ultimately towards a sect-type resistance to cultural secularization thus survived, to be (if anything) strengthened by the 1972 amalgamation of the Congregational Church of England and Wales with English Presbyterianism.

Sectarian tendencies have taken various forms. Pentecostalism has proved attractive to a small group of individuals and congregations, and some ministers and lay people have so far rejected the conventions and assumptions of the wider society as to practise Spiritual Healing. But evangelical orthodoxy has remained the usual mode of conservatism. As the character of the modern denomination might have indicated, the Secretary of the Congregational Union opposed the Billy Graham Crusade on its inaugural visit to Britain in 1954, whereas individual ministers and congregations welcomed it. From 1947, in fact, conservative evangelicalism had organized itself by establishing a Congregational Evangelical Revival Fellowship – a body considerably more conservative in outlook than the popular evangelicalism of Graham. The appointment in 1956 of the Fellowship's Secretary, Gilbert Kirby, to the post of General Secretary of the Evangelical Alliance, was evidence of the links between at least some Congregationalists and the 'shadow ecumenism' which seems to be taking shape in opposition to the mainstream denominational compromise with the secular culture. By the same logic, however, the numerical strength of the Fellowship, which has never exceeded a few hundred, reflects the general reluctance of modern Congregationalism to accept the kind of remnant mentality which resistance so often demands.

Baptists, on the other hand, have been far more willing to adopt a sectarian hostility to modern cultural values and trends. Never as deeply involved as Congregationalism in the great nineteenth-century struggles for equality, respectability and worldly acceptance, the Baptist denomination has largely retained its historic commitment to a concept of the church as a fellowship 'gathered' out of the 'world'. It has remained loyal to the idea of Christian 'separation' from dangerous or unnecessary worldly involvements, and loyal, too, to the tenets of evangelical orthodoxy. Its distinctive, demanding doctrine of Believer's Baptism may have had something to do with this characteristic conservatism. For by virtue of this symbolic act alone, entering full membership with a Baptist Church is guaranteed to remain a commitment not lightly made or easily compromised. Booth noted at the end of the nineteenth century that the commitment of the Baptist typically was something 'very deep', something 'far more intense' than the commitment of the average Congregationalist. Certainly there can be no doubt about the contemporary situation. The Baptists remain more conservative theologically than any of the other major denominations, and what Booth called 'a definite puritanism' still flourished among them much more than elsewhere.[27]

All this does not mean, as one unkind critic has put it, that a Baptist is 'a person of the opposite opinion!' The same issues which divide other Christian communities in an age of secularization also divide British Baptists. Pressures to find a 'preachable' gospel, to gain strength in union with other Churches, to retain marginal adherents by promoting a more popular, up-to-date type of image – to compromise, in short, with the contemporary *zeitgeist* – have all been evident throughout the present century. Indeed, in men like John Shakespeare, whose *The Churches at the Cross Roads* (1918) was a powerful, influential appeal for Christian re-union, and Ernest Payne, a delegate to the inaugural World Council of Churches assembly in 1948, subsequently a vice-chairman of the Council's Central Committee, a moderator of the National Free Church Council and a vice-president of the British Council of Churches, the Baptists have been represented at the highest levels of ecumenical activity in Britain. Two things, however, make this involvement different from that of the other major Free Churches.

First, Payne's ecumenical vision has evoked only minority enthusiasm within the denomination. So strong have been the tendencies towards a reactionary conservatism that when the Baptist scholar, R. L. Child, came to write a memoir in appreciation of Payne he implied, in 1967, that without such strong advocacy for continuing relations with more liberal sections of British Christianity, the Baptists might already have retreated into religious-cultural isolation. 'He has kept the future open for Baptists', Child wrote, explaining that this had been a conscious and deliberate policy in Payne's churchmanship. So critical were the decisions eventually to be taken over the problems of ecumenism and theological liberalism, that precipitate action had to be avoided despite the strength of negative feeling within the denomination. In Child's words:

Payne has never disguised his distrust of all attempts to resolve them prematurely, and has consistently maintained, in effect, that since no one knows what the church of the future will be like, we must be patient with one another and with God until he is pleased to reveal his will to us.[28]

More and more, however, Baptist opinion has hardened in the belief that an ecumenical 'church of the future' will not be a place for evangelical witness or true discipleship. At the historic Baptist Union meeting of 1926, where discussion centred on the formulation of an 'official' reply to the 'Lambeth Appeal', the essence of the Baptist position already reflected a firm, uncompromising rejection of accommodatory changes. Using the occasion to receive several papers on 'The Faith of Baptists', the meeting endorsed an exclusivist 'remnant theology' which has remained, ever since, a feature of Baptist consciousness. In a striking metaphor, a prominent theologian, J. H. Rushbrooke likened the 'true church' to the 'Ark of Salvation':

The storm could rage without, but within was security in this world and the next. But the ark was lighted only by windows that pointed heavenward. One lost sight of the world when one entered it. It is a far cry from this to the view of the modern Church. Now, it is urged, discipleship means alliance to this cause or to that, sometimes even to a political party. Is that true? To me it seems to miss the very genius of discipleship.[29]

If people like Shakespeare and Payne would have felt uneasy about such an emphasis, their very disquiet would have distinguished them from a majority of their Baptist brethren.

Their basic theology, however, would not have set them apart. For the second distinctive feature of modern Baptist religiosity is that where divergence does occur, it usually occurs *within* the limits of evangelical orthodoxy. It is a divergence of emphasis, emotional commitment or strategy, not (as in other Protestant traditions), a divergence arising from fundamental ideological discontinuities. A contrast with Anglicanism illustrates this point. In the long run both communions may have only one choice, whether to accommodate secularization or to resist it; but while at present the spectrum of opinion in the Church of England ranges from 'Christian atheism' to strict fundamentalism, among Baptists a man like Payne, of firmly evangelical views, is at the liberal end of a much narrower spectrum. Baptist interests such as that represented by the increasingly-active Baptist Revival Fellowship maintain a position which they acknowledge to be 'conservative-evangelical'; and when they refer to other Baptists as 'liberal' it is, on their own admission, chiefly to avoid 'awkward expressions' like 'non-conservative-evangelical'.[30]

## TOWARDS A NEW SECTARIANISM

As early as 1964 the Baptist Revival Fellowship was trying to alert its denomination to what loomed as an historic turning-point in British Christian history – at least in conservative evangelical minds. 'We are approaching a point of crisis in our denominational life', wrote a panel of Fellowship members in *Liberty in the Lord*, a polemic of resistance. It was a crisis, they warned fellow Baptists, 'which will involve us all in heart-searching questions and difficult decisions'. But if the decision was agonizing the issue itself was clear. It had been clarified by

Growing awareness of the 'mixed' condition of denominations and of the considerable differences over fundamental doctrines existing within them, so that the question of what is the basis for true co-operation is acutely raised.[31]

*Liberty in the Lord* was an important publication because it recognized candidly, from a denominational perspective, that traditional denominational patterns were being rendered obsolete by secularization, and because in this recognition it elaborated the feelings of conservative evangelicals in all the denominations.

But its authors went beyond the mere delineation of tensions and solidarities which cut across denominational lines. With an eye to the future, they actually listed certain tendencies which seemed to be leading evangelicalism 'towards closer outward and visible fellowship with those of like doctrinal convictions.' Three things seemed to foreshadow eventual evangelical unity – unity, that is, *against* the secular culture and *against* the liberal Protestantism which secularization has compromised. The first was a trend towards evangelical fellowship which deliberately ignored 'ecclesiastical differences', and which stressed instead 'the basis of theological essential unity'. Citing the Westminster Fellowship as a prototypical example, the authors predicted that in future spiritual and ideological solidarities would transcend 'denominational frontiers'. The second development was the emergence of the Evangelical Alliance as a focal point for evangelical organization and consultation. The third, and perhaps most striking development, was the already-impressive growth of local and regional Evangelical Fellowships which were giving a new organizational cohesion to evangelical strategies of resistance.[32]

Altering structural and cultural patterns which bear the imprimatur of centuries is no swift and easy matter. The mainstream ecumenical movement, for example, has consistently underestimated the time required to bring to fruition its schemes for Christian unity, even among liberal Protestants ready to accept far-reaching compromises. 'We dare to hope', resolved the Nottingham Faith and Order Conference of 1964, calling upon the major denominations to set a target date for the inauguration of Protestant unity in Britain, 'that this date should not be later than Easter Day, 1980'.[33] The Conference was being over-optimistic, doubtless because it could not have foreseen the breakdown of Anglican-Methodist moves towards unity. But partly because of this delay, a reactionary re-alignment of loyalties and associations among conservative evangelicals (and perhaps all evangelicals), has developed rather more slowly in the 1970s than seemed likely in the middle of the 1960s.

More important than the timing of events, however, is the fact that if British evangelicals do make their critical, seemingly-inevitable decision to opt out of the theologically liberal super-Protestantism which ecumenism seems likely to produce at some stage, the position they adopt will be essentially sectarian. They will be strongly conversionist. They will be concerned to confront the wider society, not to withdraw totally from it. Yet their effect, when successful, will be to draw people out of the secular milieu and into a religious sub-culture. Their constituency, in short, will be limited to those already alienated, for one reason or another, from the mainstream culture, and those open to persuasion to reject that culture. And their greatest danger will be the insidious temptation to modify theological and behavioural standards in the hope of wider attention and respect.

For a sect, to compromise is to invite debility. It draws strength from its suspicion of the mores and values of its social and cultural environment, for its quantitative weakness is balanced by its qualitative emphasis on intense and total loyalty from individual members, and by its 'remnant' mentality, which seeks vindication either through an (unlikely) radical transformation of the present 'world' or, failing that, through entry into a future heaven. British evangelicals, especially conservatives among them, are involved already, to a certain extent, in this kind of 'Church'-'world' relationship. When the National Assembly of Evangelicals' Commission on Evangelism made its report in 1968, even the title had a sectarian ring. *On the Other Side* was chosen deliberately, for, as the commissioners (evangelical Anglicans, Baptists, Pentecostalists and Brethren), put it

we have been mindful all the way through that the battle is supernatural. 'On the other side' of the battlefield are ranged the spiritual hosts of wickedness in heavenly places, whose subtle power and opposition will always be encountered when the Church leaves its sheltered position and challenges Satan's kingdom. This is the basic reason why there is no easy option.[34]

On the 'Lord's side', against this hostile world, there was but a remnant. The 'evangelical community', by its own admission, was 'a pathetically small minority'.[35] Ideologically, it was doomed to give 'offence' whenever it succeeded in communicating its ideas to the secular society, for its size was a reflection of its perceived oddity. Indeed, for the evangelical the future search for a 'preachable' gospel would not involve a quest for an acceptable message, but rather the reverse! There might be a need to 'remove false stumbling blocks', but only so that 'the true *skandalon* may be clearly revealed'.[36]

This is scarcely an alluring future. But even if history does prove accommodation to have been a strategy of extinction for mainstream Protestantism, a small, intense, resolute, essentially intolerant religious culture will continue to resist the secular 'world', striving to change it. For the new sectarianism to succeed in effecting any general re-conversion of post-Christian Britain would, of course, involve a reversal of profound movements of secularization and modernization – a transformation of the very essence of modern industrial society – and that is a possibility about as likely as the prospect, 2,000 years ago, that an insignificant Jewish cult might succeed in turning the great classical world upside down!

Conservative Christian minorities have often taken encouragement from this obvious analogy; and there are comforting analogies, too, in the modern age. Conservative evangelicals in the Soviet Union, a sectarian sub-culture if ever there was one, outnumber the active membership of all the British Churches combined. This is an arresting statistic, even allowing for the massive population difference between the two societies. But on closer examination, the contemporary 'Iron Curtain' sectarianism does not offer a meaningful analogy for a Christian minority looking towards the future in Britain, or indeed elsewhere in the West. The emerging secular 'world' in Britain will stultify sectarian enthusiasm, if at all, through tolerant indifference or condescending good humour; it is unlikely to stimulate sectarian tenacity through the crude brutality of a Roman arena or the more subtle persecution of a Soviet psychiatric ward. Secularization is a much deadlier foe than any previous counter-religious force in human experience.

## CATHOLICISM AT THE CROSSROADS

Catholicism has been left out at many points of the previous discussion because, in the special context of British Christianity, it is in so many ways an enigmatic force. In meeting the challenge of secularization, British Catholics have been in a unique position for several reasons. First, more than any other Christian community, their strategic responses have been dictated by the macro-strategies of global Catholicism. The Catholic Church, historically and contemporarily, has been strongest in social situations far less affected by modernization and industrialization than the great metropolitan cultures of Britain, North-West Europe and North America. Consequently, although the temptations of accommodation have been real enough, the magisterium of the Church (if not all its national hierarchies in modern Western societies), has generally maintained a hard line against ideological and moral compromise. If this has caused agony for individual Catholics in the more 'modern' cultures, and embarrassment for their intellectual leaders, it certainly has placed definite conservative constraints upon the options available to any particular branch of the Catholic universe.

Secondly, British Catholicism has been considerably insulated from the full impact of secularization by its historic and social marginality in England. A legacy of conflict and suspicion stretching from the Reformation to the fall of the Stuarts and the defeat of Jacobitism has left a deep-seated strain of anti-Catholicism in English consciousness. Notwithstanding their membership of a vast international religious community, and indeed sometimes precisely because of it, English Catholics have been made to feel and react like a sectarian sub-culture in a hostile environment. Temptations to accommodate beliefs, values and norms to such a world clearly have been reduced, not heightened, by this latent yet pervasive disapproval. And in the past century-and-a-quarter, while the historical animosities have lost their original relevance, the bitterness has been kept alive by the increasingly 'Irish' character of English Catholicism. Massive Irish migration to Britain has been a continuing feature of this long period, and while Irish numbers have increased the quantitative strength of the Church in vast degree, they have at the same time reinforced the somewhat alien image which might otherwise have faded. For the Irish, as John Bright put it more than a century ago, Catholicism tends to be 'not only a faith, but absolutely a patriotism'.[37]

Thus in its Irishness British, and, even more, English Catholicism, has both a clientele less susceptible than most other sections of the modern society to feel acutely the pressures of cultural secularization, and a public image associating it with a 'patriotism' not apt to evoke ready acceptance from the British mind. The result has been clear self-awareness of limits to the ability of Catholicism to influence the British environment, limits which, ironically, leave this small section of a global Church, in its own 'world', more like a 'sect' than a 'church'. De la Bedoyere stated the realistic view almost forty years ago. Noting

T. S. Eliot's belief that only the Church of England was in a position to realize 'the idea of a Christian society' in England, he agreed that,

short of some very unexpected event taking place in the spiritual order, the Catholic Church in England could not realize this society within measurable time . . .[38]

Acceptance of a backstage role in British religion, of marginality in British society and relative isolation from the mainstream of British culture has been reflected in theological conservatism and uncompromising morality. When in 1960 D. H. Lawrence's *Lady Chatterley's Lover* was challenged in court under the Obscene Publications Act, Anglican bishops and other prominent Protestants took their places as 'experts' for the defence. When a Catholic layman, W. St John-Stevas, joined them, he was censured in the pages of the *Catholic Times*.[39] Resistance, not accommodation, was the norm. The social teaching of the Church, the *Catholic Times* had conceded a few years earlier, 'ran counter' to the prevailing values of socialists and liberal-capitalists alike, and the result was that in modern British society at large Catholicism was 'largely rejected or ignored'.[40] On the credit side, however, marginality and conservatism were defences against secularization. In its social and cultural orientation Catholicism displayed the strengths and weaknesses of a sect, for if it had but minimal influence on its 'world' it retained the loyalty of its adherents to a degree which most Protestant denominations might have envied. As an Anglican convert put it, conversion to Catholicism meant the 'way of the Cross'. It required submission to a supernatural authority. It involved 'severe self-denial in the acceptance of extremely difficult moral principles'.[41]

The question remains, however, how long such a religious culture can resist the corrosive effects of secularization. With an air of smugness, Catholic observers have often remarked on the evolution of liberal Protestantism, citing it as an example of the contentless superficiality produced in the absence of uncompromising religious authority. It may be, however, that the smugness has been premature. Peter Berger, the American sociologist, has speculated that, 'in a very real way . . . the Protestant development is prototypical, to the point that one can even say that quite possibly all other religious traditions in the modern situation may be predestined to go through varieties of the Protestant experience'. The possibility that Protestantism, and particularly its 'crisis of theology', may turn out to have been a 'dress rehearsal' for the decline of all religion in a modern milieu, is argued by Berger in terms of the 'peculiar relationship' of the major Protestant traditions to 'the genesis and inner character of the modern world'. For the fact that Protestantism has felt the full force of secularization earlier

155

does not imply that Catholicism, in the long run, will feel it any less.[42]

In the aftermath of Vatican II, the historic Council called by pope John XXIII, Catholicism did in fact seem to have set out on the road which Protestantism had taken earlier in its search for accommodation with the secular culture. The motivation had been comparable. John XXIII, an English Catholic scholar observed in 1966, had seen most clearly 'the failure of the Church to reach the unbelieving world'. He wanted a measure of accommodation, including a reformulation of dogma, so that the Church would cease to appear 'a museum of ancient artefacts'.[43] The ensuing discussions precipitated a crisis in the conservative world of British Catholicism. Archbishop Heenan stated publicly that the Pope seemed to have been 'bewildered by the Council', and was promptly accused of having a 'Back to the ghetto' mentality![44]

Looking back in 1976, a Joint Working Party on Pastoral Strategy, set up five years earlier by the Catholic Bishops' Conference and the National Conference of Priests, pointed out that after Vatican II British Catholics had faced particular problems. 'In thinking and practice', the Working Party reported,

the local church had been only distantly in touch with continental scholarship, theological and liturgical development and practical application.[45]

The challenge of secularization had thus struck suddenly, and as in Protestant movements similarly challenged, the danger had arisen of 'polarization under categories like "progressive" and "traditional" '.[46] But Catholic strategy suddenly changed. On the accommodatory matter of dogmatic reformulation, for example, John XXIII's successor, Paul VI, revived the conservative principle that traditional definitions 'are adapted to men of all times'. His encyclicals *Mysterium Fidei* and *Humanae Vitae* expressed a Catholic reversion to a traditional reactionary attitude to secularization, and despite radical hopes and agitations, Pope John Paul II seems no less hostile than Paul VI to a Catholic rapprochment with modern Western civilization.

It may be that the strength of Catholicism outside the centres of modern culture will deliver it from the harsh dilemmas which secularization has imposed upon British Protestantism. Perhaps it will continue to 'leaven' the secular 'world' without capitulating to areligious beliefs and values; and, if so, it will have an advantage over both liberal Protestantism and a new Protestant sectarianism in the decades ahead. But if its evolution is dictated by the 'Church'-'world' relationships of the modern industrial situation no safeguards of tradition or authority seem capable of securing it against some version of the Protestant fate. For unless there is to be some catastrophic breakdown of modern industrial society – an event not inconceivable in the early 1980s – the social and psychological pressures of modernization will continue to secularize an already 'post-Christian' society.

# NOTES

1. Murchland, B. (1967), p. 14.
2. Edwards, D. L. (1963), p. 107.
3. Kee, A. (1971).
4. Berger, P. (1969), p. 163.
5. Currie, R., Gilbert, A. D. and Horsley, L. H. (1977), pp. 158–60.
6. Mullen, R. (1967), pp. 222–32.
7. Van den Heuval, A. H. (1966), pp. 103–7.
8. Ibid., p. 98.
9. Ibid., p. 99.
10. *On the Other Side* (1968), p. 84.
11. Ibid., p. 85.
12. Browne, M. K. (1979), *passim*.
13. Watkin, E. I. (1966), p. 287.
14. W. Nicholls, in Paton, D. M. (1958), p. 24.
15. In Harvey, G. L. H. (1936), p. xv.
16. In Harvey, G. L. H. (1936), p. xv.
17. Towler, R. (1969), p. 113.
18. 'An Analysis of Sect Development', *American Sociological Review* (1959), **24**:1, p. 6. Quoted by Towler, Ibid., p. 118.
19. *Annual Report of the General Assembly of the Presbyterian Church in Ireland*, 1971, pp. 162–75.
20. Ibid., p. 148.
21. Ibid., p. 165.
22. Robinson, J. A. T. (1963), p. 7.
23. Davidson, N. (1965), p. 65.
24. Ibid., p. 331.
25. Booth, C. (1903), p. 111.
26. *Congregational Quarterly*, XV (January 1937), pp. 113–14.
27. Booth, C. (1903), p. 128.
28. Champion, E. L. (1967), p. 8.
29. Rushbrooke, J. H. *et. al.* (1926), p. 55.
30. Bamber, T. M. (1964), pp. 3, 33.
31. Ibid., p. 33.
32. Ibid., pp. 33–4.
33. Edwards, D. L. (1973), p. 52.
34. *On the Other Side* (1968), p. 179.
35. Ibid., p. 153.
36. Clark, N., 'The Crisis of Biblical Theology', in Champion, E. L. (1967), p. 94.

37. Bright, J. (1866), p. 369.
38. De la Bedoyere, M. (n.d.), p. 178-9.
39. *Catholic Times*, 11 November 1960.
40. Ibid., 17 May 1957.
41. Ibid., 7 June 1957.
42. Berger, P. (1969), pp. 155-6.
43. Quoted by Lubbock, Y., 'Belief is Being: Thoughts on the Survival of Christian Belief', in de la Bedoyere (1966), p. 39.
44. Ibid., pp. 39-40.
45. *A Time for Building* (1976), p. 13.
46. Ibid., p. 14.

# Bibliographical note

A standard bibliography is not really feasible in a study which has touched on themes as broad and chronological distances as extensive as those involved in the foregoing chapters. The historical approach to secularization not only trepasses into many areas of social, economic and cultural history, but also crosses boundaries into sociology, anthropology, philosophy and religious studies. The materials illuminating its many facets are therefore almost inexhaustible. Readers wanting bibliographical guidance will find in the list of works cited as references an indication of the kinds of sources which have been used to develop the particular arguments of this book. But perhaps the best bibliographical advice to general readers is to stress the obvious, major contributions to the literature, for familiarity with such contributions automatically increases a reader's bibliographical awareness and expertise. Scholars already well-versed in the field will of course carry their own bibliographical maps with them.

Sociologically, the vanguard of scholarly study of secularization in Britain is dominated by Bryan Wilson, David Martin, and the students and colleagues who work with them. Wilson's *Religion in Secular Society: A Sociological Comment* (Watts, London, 1966), or his fascinating Riddell Lectures, published as *Contemporary Transformations of Religion* (O.U.P., London, 1976), make excellent starting-points for the historian, but at the same time no amount of expertise renders their insights superfluous. The same kind of thing can be said of Martin's *A Sociology of English Religion* (Heinemann, London, 1967), his *The Religious and the Secular: Studies in Secularization* (Routledge, London, 1969), and of the work which he and Michael Hill have done as editors of the series, *A Sociological Yearbook of Religion in Britain,* 1-8 (SCM, London, 1968-75). Martin's more recent study, *A General Theory of*

*Secularization* (Blackwell, Oxford, 1978) appeared too late, at least in Australia, to influence the thinking behind the present inquiry, but its ambitious synoptic approach to the elaboration of secularization theory in the light of recent evidence about the development of European religion makes it a contribution of considerable significance. Finally, the historian interested in secularization will find useful theoretical leads, and an interesting discussion of various kinds of evidence, in M. J. Jackson's *The Sociology of Religion: Theory and Practice* (Batsford, London, 1974).

The history of secularization, certainly to the extent that it is distinguishable from sociological approaches, remains very much in its infancy. Owen Chadwick's *The Secularization of the European Mind in the Nineteenth Century* (C.U.P., Cambridge, 1975), and Susan Budd's *Varieties of Unbelief: Atheists and Agnostics in English Society* (Heinemann, London, 1977), are good recent examples of the one field within the general area which has received considerable attention – the phenomenon of ideological secularization. Social aspects of the history, although receiving little direct attention, have been raised, and often most usefully explored, in a growing number of recent studies concentrating less on traditional religious history than on relationships between religion and society. Such works include: R. Currie, *Methodism Divided: A Study in the Sociology of Ecumenicalism* (Faber, London, 1968), A. D. Gilbert, *Religion and Society in Industrial England* (Longman, London, 1976), H. McLeod, *Class and Religion in the Late Victorian City* (Croom Helm, London, 1974), E. R. Norman, *Church and Society in England, 1770-1970* (Clarendon, Oxford, 1976), and S. Yeo, *Religion and Voluntary Organizations in Crisis* (Croom Helm, London, 1976). A mass of relevant material is, of course, unavailable except in the primary sources, or in the general ecclesiastical and denominational histories which focus on secularization, if at all, only from the limited perspective of religious organizations themselves. But bibliographical information on such sources is readily available.

Theologians, church leaders and journalists have produced a mass of material on secularization, much of it partisan, some of it ephemeral. W. Nicholls' *Systematic and Philosophical Theology* (Penguin, Harmondsworth, 1969), remains a good general introduction to trends in modern Christian theology. Christopher Driver's *A Future for the Free Churches* (SCM London, 1962), although somewhat dated, is still a stimulating, journalistic exploration of the decline of the Free Churches; and among the better examples of partisan discussion, David L. Edward's *Religion and Change* (Hodder and Stoughton, London, 1969) and Os Guinness's *The Dust of Death* (I.V.F., Downers Grove, Ill., 1973) are outstanding for their breadth and understanding. An examination of the foregoing argument will, of course, indicate the debts which it owes to the tragically-undeveloped ideas which Dietrich Bonhoeffer was beginning to explore in his prison correspondence of 1944 and 1945. But, as in most studies of religion in the modern world, the most profound influence of all has been the work of Max Weber, and there can be no better way to conclude a bibliographical note on secularization than to stress that any inquiry cannot but be enriched by an early and detailed acquaintance with Weber's *The Sociology of Religion* (various edns), *The Protestant Ethic and the Spirit of Capitalism* (various edns), and indeed with all his work on modernization, rationalization and the 'disenchantment' of the modern world.

# References

Arnold, M. (1895), *Letters, 1848–1888*, vol. IV (ed. G. W. E. Russell), Macmillan, London.

*A Time for Building: Report of the Joint Working Party on Pastoral Strategy* (1976), Catholic Information Services, Abbots Langley, Herts.

Babbage, C. (1835), *On the Economy of Manufactures*, London.

Bamber, T. M. *et al.* (1964), *Liberty in the Lord: Comment on Trends in Baptist Thought Today*, Baptist Revival Fellowship, London.

Basalla, G., Coleman, W. and Kargon, R. H. (eds) (1970), *Victorian Science*, Doubleday, N.Y.

Bedoyere, M. de la (n.d.), *Christian Crisis*, Burns Oates and Washbourne, London.

Bedoyere, M. de la (1966), *The Future of Catholic Christianity*, Constable, London.

Bell, C. and Newby, H. (eds) (1974), *The Sociology of Community: A Selection of Readings*, Cass, London.

Berger, P. (1961), *The Noise of Solemn Assemblies*, Doubleday, N.Y.

Berger, P. (1967), 'A Sociological View of the Secularization of Theology', *Journal of the Scientific Study of Religion*, VI:1 (spring).

Berger, P. (1969), *The Social Reality of Religion*, Faber, London.

Bonhoeffer, D. (1953), *Letters and Papers from Prison* (ed. E. Bethge, trans. R. H. Fuller), SCM, London.

Booth, C. (1903), *Life and Labour of the People in London*, 3rd. Series, vol. 7, Macmillan, London.

Bossy, J. (1970), 'The Counter-Reformation and the People of Catholic Europe', *Past and Present*, **47**.

Bossy, J. (1977), 'Holiness and Society', *Past and Present*, **75**, pp. 119-37.

Brennan, T., Cooney, E. W. and Pollins, M. (1954), *Social Change in South-West Wales*, Watts, London.

Briggs, A. (1959), *The Age of Improvement*, Longman, London.

Bright, J. (1866), *Speeches*, vol. I, London.

Browne, M. K. (1979), 'The Idea of a Christian Social Order: Aspects of Anglican Social Thought in England, 1918–1945', unpublished Ph.D thesis, Australian National University.

Burckhardt, J. (1944), *The Civilisation of the Renaissance in Italy* (trans. S.G.C. Middlemore), Allen and Unwin, London.

Burke, E. (1909), *Reflections on the Revolution in France* (ed. C. W. Eliot), Collier, N.Y.

Campbell, C. (1972), 'The Cult, the Cultic Milieu and Secularization', in M. Hill (ed.), *A Sociological Yearbook of Religion in Britain*, 5, SCM, London.

Cannon, W. F. (1964), 'The normative role of science in early Victorian thought', *Journal of the History of Ideas*, **25**.

Carlton, E. (1968), ' "The Call": The Concept of Vocation in the Free Church Ministry', in D. Martin (ed.), *A Sociological Yearbook of Religion in Britain*, 1, SCM, London.

Chadwick, O. (1970), *The Victorian Church*, Vol. II, Adam and Charles Black, London.

Champion, E. L. (1967), *Outlook for Christianity*, Lutterworth, London.

Cipolla, C. (1962), *The Economic History of World Population*, Pelican, Harmondsworth.

Clark, G. K. (1965), *The Making of Victorian England*, Methuen, London.

Currie, R. (1968), *Methodism Divided: A Study in the Sociology of Ecumenicalism*, Faber, London.

Currie, R., Gilbert, A. D. and Horsley, H. (1977), *Churches and Churchgoers: Patterns of Church Growth in the British Isles since 1700*, Clarendon, Oxford.

Dale, A. W. W. (1902), *The Life of R. W. Dale of Birmingham*, Independent, London.

Davidson, N. (1965), *Reflections of a Scottish Churchman*, Hodder and Stoughton, London.

Davies, E. T. (1965), *Religion in the Industrial Revolution in South Wales*, Univ. of Wales Press, Cardiff.

Davies, H. (1965), *Worship and Theology in England*, Vol. V: *The Ecumenical Century*, Princeton Univ. Press, Princeton.

Dawson, C. (1945), *Progress and Religion*, Sheed and Ward, London.

Deane, P. and Cole, W. A. (1962), *British Economic Growth, 1688–1959*, C.U.P., Cambridge.

Edwards, D. L. (1963), *The Honest to God Debate*, SCM, London.

Edwards, D. L. (1973), *The British Churches Turn to the Future*, SCM, London.

*References*

Evenett, H. O. (1968), *The Spirit of the Counter-Reformation* (ed. J. Bossy), C.U.P., Cambridge.

Eversley, D. C. (1967), 'The Home Market and Economic Growth in England, 1750–80', in E. L. Jones and G. E. Mingay (eds), *Land, Labour and Population in the Industrial Revolution*, Edward Arnold, London.

Feuchtwanger, E. J. (1975), *Gladstone*, Allen Lane, London.

Feuerbach, L. (1854), *Essence of Christianity* (trans. G. Eliot), London.

Gay, J. D. (1971), *The Geography of Religion in England*, Duckworth, London.

Gerth, H. H. and Mills, C. W. (1946), *From Max Weber: Essays in Sociology*, Random, N.Y.

Gilbert A. D. (1976), *Religion and Society in Industrial England*, Longman, London.

Gilmore, A. (ed.) (1971), *Ministry in Question*, Longman, Darton and Todd, London.

Gorer, G. (1965), *Death, Grief and Mourning*, Cresset Press, London.

Green, R. W. (1959), *Protestantism and Capitalism: The Weber Thesis and its Critics*, D. C. Heath, Lexington.

Greene, J. C. (1963), *Darwin and the Modern World View*, Mentor, N.Y.

Halsey, A. H., (ed.) (1972), *Trends in British Society since 1900*, Macmillan, London.

Hardwick, J. C. (1930), *Institutional Religion*, Benn, London.

Harvey, G. L. H. (ed.) (1936), *The Church in the Twentieth Century*, Macmillan, London.

Hazard, P. (1973), *The European Mind 1680–1715* (trans. J. L. May), Penguin, Harmondsworth.

Hughes, E. C. (1936), 'The Ecological Aspects of Institutions', *American Sociological Review*, **I**.

Hughes, H. S. (1959), *Consciousness and Society*, MacGibbon and Kee, London.

Huxley, A. (1928), *Point Counter Point*, Chatto and Windus, London.

Independent Television Authority (1970), *Religion in Britain and Northern Ireland*, I.T.A., London.

Inglis, K. S. (1963), *Churches and the Working Classes in Victorian England*, Routledge, London.

Inkeles, A. (1969), 'Making Men Modern', *American Journal of Sociology*, **75**:2.

Johnson, W., Whyman, J. and Wykes, G. (1967), *A Short Economic and Social History of Twentieth Century Britain*, Allen and Unwin, London.

Jones, I. G. (1961), 'The Liberation Society and Welsh Politics, 1844–1868', *Welsh History Review*, **1**:2.

Jones, V. (1969), *The Church in a Mobile Society*, Christopher Davies, Swansea.

Jung, C. G. (1953), *Psychology and Alchemy*, in R. F. C. Hull (ed.) *The Collected Works of C. G. Jung*, Vol. 12, Routledge, London.

Kee, A. (1971) *The Way of Transcendence*, Penguin, Harmondsworth.

Koss, S. (1975), *Nonconformity in Modern British Politics*, Batsford, London.

Koyré, A. (1968), *From the Closed World to the Infinite Universe*, Vintage, Baltimore.

Lacqueur, T. W. (1976), *Religion and Respectability: Sunday Schools and Working-Class Culture, 1780–1850*, Yale Univ. Press, New Haven.

Mackintosh, W. H. (1972), *Disestablishment and Liberation: the Movement for the Seperation of the Anglican Church from State Control*, Epworth, London.

Mandrou, R. (1978), *From Humanism to Science, 1480–1700*, Pelican, Harmondsworth.

Marcuse, H. (1968), *One-Dimensional Man*, Sphere Books, London.

Martin, D. (1967), *A Sociology of English Religion*, Heinemann, London.

Martin, D. (1979), 'Revs and Revolutions: Church Trends and Theological Fashions', *Encounter*, LII (January).

Mathias, P. (1972), 'Who Unbound Prometheus? Science and Technical Change 1600–1800', in Mathias (ed.) *Science and Society, 1600–1900*, C.U.P., Cambridge.

McLeod, H. (1974), *Class and Religion in the Late Victorian City*, Croom Helm, London.

Mitchell, B. R. and Deane, P. (1962), *Abstract of British Historical Statistics*, C.U.P., Cambridge.

Morgan, K. O. (1970), *Wales in British Politics, 1868–1922*, 2nd. edn, Univ. of Wales Press, Cardiff.

Mudie-Smith, R. (1904), *The Religious Life of London*, Hodder and Stoughton, London.

Mullen, R. (1967), *The Mormons*, W. H. Allen, London.

Murchland, B. (1967), *The Meaning of the Death of God*, Random, N.Y.

Murphy, H. R. (1955), 'The Ethical Revolt Against Christian Orthodoxy in Early Victorian England', *American Historical Review*, LX.

Neibuhr, R. (1941), *The Nature and Destiny of Man*, 2 vols., Nisbet, London.

Neibuhr, A. Richard (1957), *The Social Sources of Denominationalism*, Meridan, Cleveland.

# References

Nicholls, W. (1969), *Systematic and Philosophical Theology*, Pelican, Harmondsworth.

*On the Other Side* (1968), 'Report of the Evangelical Alliance's Commission on Evangelism', Scripture Union, London.

Oswald, J. (1768), *An Appeal to Common Sense in Behalf of Religion*, 2nd. edn, London.

Paton, D. M. (ed.) (1958), *Essays in Anglican Self-Criticism*, SCM, London.

Paul, L. (1964), *The Deployment and Payment of the Clergy*, Church Information Office, London.

Perkin, H. (1969) *The Origins of Modern English Society, 1780–1880*, Routledge, London.

Pickering, W. S. F. (1968), 'Religion – a Leisure-time Pursuit?', *A Sociological Yearbook of Religion in Britain*, 1, SCM, London.

Pyke, M. (1967), *The Science Century*, John Murray, London.

Ramsden, W. E. (1971), 'Geographical vs. Functional Community: A Problem of Identity', *Religion in Life*, **XL**:2 (Summer).

Rattansi, P. M. (1972), 'The Social Interpretation of Science in the Seventeenth Century', in P. Mathias, (ed.), *Science and Society 1600–1900*, C.U.P., Cambridge.

Robertson, H.M. (1933), *Aspects of the Rise of Economic Individualism*, C.U.P., Cambridge.

Robinson, J. A. T. (1963), *Honest to God*, SCM, London.

Rowntree, B. S. and Lavers, B. R. (1951), *English Life and Leisure*, Longman, London.

Royle, E. (1971), *Radical Politics 1790–1900: Religion and Unbelief*, Longman, London.

Rushbrooke, J. H. *et al.* (1926), *The Faith of Baptists: Papers on Belief and Polity, being the substance of Addresses delivered at the Assembly of the Baptist Union . . . Leeds, May 1926*, Kingsgate Press, London.

Samuelsson, K. (1961), *Religion and Economic Action* (trans. E. G. French), Heinemann, London.

Santillana, G. (1956), *The Age of Adventure*, Mentor, N.Y.

Semmel, B. (1974), *The Methodist Revolution*, Heinemann, London.

Singer, C. (1959), *A Short History of Scientific Ideas*, Clarendon, Oxford.

Smith, A. (1909), *The Wealth of Nations* (ed. C. J. Bullock), Collier, N.Y.

Smith, B. J. (1898), *Why are we Independents?* Independent, London.

Soloway, R. A. (1969), *Prelates and People: Ecclesiastical Social Thought in England, 1783–1852*, Routledge, London.

Sombart, W. (1915), *The Quintessence of Capitalism*, Dutton, N.Y.

Specialised Ministries (1971), *The Report of a Working Party of the Ministry Committee of the Advisory Council for the Church's Ministry on priests in specialised work*, Church Information Office, London.

St. Clair, W. (1840), *Popular View of Life Assurance*, London.

Stephen, L. (1873), *Essays in Free Thinking and Plain Speaking*, London.

Tawney, R. H. (1938), *Religion and the Rise of Capitalism*, Pelican, Harmondsworth.

Thomas, K. (1973), *Religion and the Decline of Magic*, Penguin, Harmondsworth.

Thompson, E. J. (1976), *Social Trends*, HMSO, London.

Thompson, E. P. (1968), *The Making of the English Working Class*, 2nd. edn, Pelican, Harmondsworth.

Thompson, E. P. (1974), 'Patrician Society, Plebeian Culture', *Journal of Social History*, 7:4.

Thompson, J. A. (1969), *The Collapse of the British Liberal Party*, D. C. Heath, Lexington.

Towler, R. (1969), 'Puritan and Antipuritan: Types of Vocation to the Ordained Ministry', *A Sociological Yearbook of Religion in Britain*, 2, SCM, London.

Toynbee, A. (1968), 'Changing Attitudes towards Death in the Modern World', in Toynbee *et. al.* (eds), *Man's Concern with Death*, Hodder and Stoughton, London.

Trevor-Roper, H. (1967), *Religion, the Reformation and Social Change, and other Essays*, Macmillan, London.

Ullmann, W. (1965), *A History of Political Thought: The Middle Ages*, Penguin, Harmondsworth.

Van den Heuval, A. H. (1966), *The Humiliation of the Church*, SCM, London.

Vincent, J. (1966), *The Formation of the Liberal Party, 1857–1868*, Constable, London.

Ward, W. R. (1965), 'The Tithe Question in England in the Early Nineteenth Century', *Journal of Ecclesiastical History*, **XVI**:1 (April).

Ward, W. R. (1972), *Religion and Society in England, 1790–1850*, Batsford, London.

Watkin, E. I. (1966), 'The Wisdom of the Spirit: A Platonist's Faith', in M. de la Bedoyere (ed.), *The Future of Catholic Christianity*, Constable, London.

Watson, G. (1973), *The English Ideology*, Allen Lane, London.

Weber, M. (1958), *The City* (trans. D. Martindale and G. Neuwirth), Free Press, Glencoe, N.Y.

Weber, M. (1930), *The Protestant Ethic and the Spirit of Capitalism* (trans. T. Parsons), Allen and Unwin, London.

Wesley, J. (1876), *Sermons of Several Occasions*, 3 vols., London.

### References

Whyte, A. G. (1949), *The Story of the Rationalist Press Association*, Watts, London.

Wood, A. S. (1960), *The Inextinguishable Blaze*, Paternoster Press, London.

Yates, R. (1815), *The Church in Danger: a Statement of the cause, and of the possible means of averting that danger attempted . . .*, London.

Yeo, S. (1976), *Religion and Voluntary Organizations in Crisis*, Croom Helm, London.

# Index

# Index

'Church'–'Chapel' relations, 72–6, 87
Church Defence Associations, 75
Church of England, xi, 70–5, 81, 85, 88, 108, 110, 112–15, 117–19, 127–9, 140–5, 147, 152, 155
*Church of England Newspaper*, 115
Church growth, x, xii, 76–80, 95–6, 109, 128–30, 136
Church membership, 76–80, 95–6, 105, 109, 111, 122, 129–30, 136
Church of Scotland, 116, 128, 145–6
*Church Times*, 115
'Church' and 'world' relationship, xii, xiv, 25, 29, 66, 69, 90, 102–3, 105, 109, 112–13, 117, 119, 121, 123–5, 127, 133, 138, 140, 145–6, 152, 155–6
Civil War, 35
Clark, G. Kitson, 74
Clark, Neville, 117
Class, 51, 55, 69, 97: and religion, 72, 74, 79, 86–95, 103, 114–15; and community, 91; proletarian, 55, 79, 86–95, 113; and secularization, 86–91
Clement VI, Pope, 24
Clergy, 25, 70–1, 75, 77, 84–7, 93, 96, 111, 113–19, 124, 126, 128, 130, 136, 141, 144, 147–8
Cobb, John, B., 133
Cocks, H. F. Lovell, 147
Community, 62, 69, 80–5, 91–2, 110, 114
Congregationalism, 73, 78, 107, 110–11, 116, 119–20, 129, 147–9
Consciousness, xii, 6, 8, 11, 13–15, 19, 21, 25–6, 30–1, 36–7, 43, 47, 53, 56–7, 59–60, 62, 64–6, 68, 83, 88, 91, 108, 135–7: religious, xiii, 5, 9–10, 12–13, 17–19, 23–4, 31, 33, 38, 48, 60, 62, 64–5, 68–9, 137; secular, xiv, 9–11, 13, 18–19, 23, 31, 33, 38–9, 45, 48, 55, 60, 119, 123, 133, 137
Conservative Party, 87–8, 96–7
Copernicus, 34
Cromwell, 55
Currie, Robert, x, 126, 128

Dale, R. W., 107
Darwin, Charles, 58
Davidson, Nevile, 117, 146
Davies, E. T., 90
De la Bedoyere, Michael, 103, 154
Death, 49, 52–3, 61–3, 137
Denominational religion, 102–4, 106–7, 109–11, 122–3, 125–6, 128–9, 133, 135–6, 138, 140–3, 147, 149, 151
Disease, 49, 52, 61
Disenchantment, 9–10, 14, 18, 39

Dissent, 144: Old Dissent, 72; New Dissent, 73, 79, 82, 89, 93
Durkheim, Emile, 68

Ecumenism, x, 73, 113, 125–30, 133, 138–42, 144–5, 148–52
Edwards, David L., 129–30
Elim Foursquare Gospel Alliance, 141
Eliot, T. S., xi, xii, 155
England, 1, 25, 30–2, 53, 70–1, 73, 75, 77, 87, 90, 92, 128, 142, 144–8, 154
Enlightenment, 17, 20, 23, 26, 33–8, 42, 47, 54
Erasmus, 23
*Essays and Reviews*, 120
Ethical Union, 56
Europe, 1, 4, 20–2, 24–6, 34–6, 145
Evangelical Alliance, 139–40, 142, 144, 148, 151
Evangelical Revival, 79
Evangelicals, evangelicalism, 7, 72–3, 110, 118, 120, 130, 138–45, 147–53

Famine, 49
Fascism, 5
Feuerbach, L. 6, 38
First World War, 74, 76–7, 79, 83, 87, 90, 120, 127
Franck, Sebastian, 29
Franklin, Benjamin, 33
French Revolution, 37

Galileo, 23, 34
Gibbon, Edward, 19
Gilmore, Alec, 116
Gladstone, W. E. 87–8
God, 5–6, 11–12, 18, 23–4, 28–9, 31–2, 38, 41, 59–62, 108, 117–18, 121–2, 125, 130, 133, 139
Gorer, Geoffrey, 62–3
Graham, Billy, 148

Hardwicke, J. C., 94
Hazard, Paul, 35
Hedonism, 33, 61, 92
Heenan, Cardinal John, 130, 134, 139, 156
Hoggart, Richard, 91
Holyoake, G. J., 55
*Honest to God*, 121–3, 133, 146
Hughes, H. P., 107
*Humanae Vitae*, 156
Humanism, 20–1, 24, 34, 120: Christian, 21; secular, 33–8, 42, 120, 137
Hume, David, 35
Hus, 25

170

171

## Index

Presbyterian Church of Ireland, 144–6
Presbyterian Church of Wales, 90, 144–6
Presbyterianism, 76, 96, 144–6: Scottish, 76–7, 87, 128, 144–6; Welsh, 112, 144–5; Irish, 76, 144–6; English, 77, 129, 148
Primitive Methodism, 82, 89
Privatization, 96–8
Protestantism, 26–34, 72, 76–9, 124–5, 134, 138, 140, 142, 144, 152–3, 155–7
'Puritans', 118–19: cf. 'Anti-Puritans'
Puritanism, 28–33
Pyke, Magnus, 61

Quasi-Religious Phenomena, 4, 7

Radio, 85, 97, 121
Rationalist Press Association, 56
Rationality, 63–6
Rationalization, 14, 18, 30–1, 34, 39, 45, 63
Redundancy, xi, xii
Reformation, 26–8, 33–4, 70, 93, 154
Religion, xii–xiii, 19, 26, 28–9, 31, 38–9, 49, 60, 62, 64, 80, 116–18, 121–2: decline of, xii, 1–4, 8, 10, 14–15, 38–9, 69; definition of, xv, 2, 4–10, 12–13, 15, 68; history of, xiii, xiv, 10, 64; virtuoso, 29–30; and science, 58–9; and politics, 86–91
Religious institutions, xiv, 3–5, 14, 68–9, 71, 73–4, 93, 95
Religious organizations, xiii, 3, 5, 14, 68–9, 75, 77–9, 84–5, 91, 93, 102, 111, 126, 146
Religious revivals, 74–5, 112
Renaissance, 17, 20–6, 34, 39, 92
Revolution of 1688, 35
Ritschl, Albrecht, 11
Ritual, 4–5, 9, 24, 62–3, 68
Robinson, J. A. T., 121–3, 134, 143, 146
Rowntree, Seebohm, 96, 122
Royal Society, 57
Rushbrooke, J. H., 150

Salutati, Coluccio, 21
Salvation, 11–13, 27
Salvationism, 47, 49–50, 64
Save Britain's Heritage Movement, xi
Schleiermacher, Friedrich, 119–21
Scholasticism, 23
Science, 14, 22, 33–4, 35, 41, 52, 56–61, 119–20, 141: scientism, 56–61
Scotland, 70, 76–7, 90, 116, 144–5
Second World War, 77, 97, 112, 121, 128, 135, 140

Sectarianism, x, 27–8, 78, 94–5, 104–5, 109, 133, 135–7, 140, 142–3, 145–8, 150–6
Secular culture, 9, 34, 36, 47–67 *passim*, 103, 110, 119, 121–2, 147–8, 156
Secularism, 38, 54–6, 60
Secularization, x, xii–xv, 1–4, 6–15, 17–18, 20, 22–4, 30–2, 34, 44–5, 55, 58–63, 66, 69, 72–3, 76–81, 83, 88, 91–2, 102–4, 106, 124, 127–30, 133–4, 136–8, 141, 145–7, 149–53, 155: institutional, 14, 45, 73–4, 77, 85–98, 106, 110–11, 113, 116, 127; history of, xv, 8, 10, 13–15, 17, 26, 32–3, 36, 43, 70, 73–4; cultural, 20, 39, 48, 59–60, 69, 72, 75–6, 78, 113, 127, 140, 148, 159; and politics, 86–91; of the Church, 78–9, 102, 105–30 *passim*, 141, 148
Seventh-Day Adventists, 156
Shakespeare, John, 149–50
Shaw, G. B., 47
Sikhs, 15
Simpson, James, 52
Smith, Adam, 51, 65
Southey, Robert, 81
Sport and recreation, xii, 7, 92–8 *passim*, 110
Spurgeon, Charles H., 107
Stephens, Sir James, 60–1
Stephens, Leslie, 59–60
Supernatural, The, 5–13, 18, 23, 30–2, 50, 60, 64–6, 68, 144, 152, 155
Supernaturalism, 37, 108
Superstition, 4, 6–7, 28, 30–1, 37

Taylor, A. J. P., 2
Television, 8, 51, 62, 65–6, 91, 96–8, 121
Theology, x, xii, 3, 6–7, 12, 17–18, 23, 26–8, 30–2, 38, 58–60, 66, 69, 102, 107–8, 117, 119–25 *passim*, 130, 133–5, 138–41, 143, 147–9, 152, 155
'Thinkers Library', 56
Thomas, Keith, 49
Thompson, E. P., 86, 89, 93
Tillich, Paul, 121
*Times, The*, xi, xv n.
Toland, John, 35
Towler, Robert, 118, 143
Trade Unionism, 89–90
Transcendence, 5, 11, 18, 28, 30–1, 37, 64, 125, 134
Treacy, Eric, ix
Trevor, John, 89

Ullmann, Walter, 25
United Free Church of Scotland, 77
United Methodist Free Churches, 127

172